the gilded room

the gilded room

DECORATING with METALLIC EFFECTS,
from METAL LEAF to POWDERS, PASTES & PAINTS

kerry skinner

David & Charles

A DAVID & CHARLES BOOK

First published in the UK in 2000

Text copyright © Kerry Skinner 2000
Photography and layout Copyright © David & Charles 2000

A catalogue record for this book is available from the British Library.

ISBN 0 7153 1140 9

Commissioning editor   Lindsay Porter
Art direction and design   Ali Myer
Text editor   Beverley Jollands
Photography   Tim France
Styling   Kerry Skinner
Assistant Editor   Jennifer Proverbs

Printed in France by Pollina
for David & Charles
Brunel House, Newton Abbot, Devon

The author has made every effort to ensure that all the instructions in this book
are accurate and safe, and therefore cannot accept liability for any resulting injury,
damage or loss to persons or property however it may arise.

contents

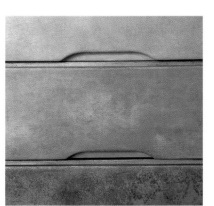

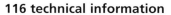

introduction

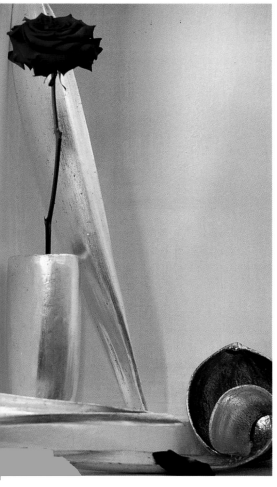

Transfer leaf can be applied to many surfaces. Here, the original objects are made of wood and other organic materials.

My usual decorating philosophy – less is more – suggests that you should keep projects simple. If you can find an easy way to fulfil your creative intent, you should use it: if the technique becomes too dominant the spontaneity and your enjoyment of the work may suffer. But gilding turns this theory on its head. Its traditional techniques are tried and tested, and if you ignore them the results will be disappointing. But don't be daunted; with practice and experiment you will not only achieve beautiful and unique results, but will have the satisfaction of acquiring a time-honoured skill. And while some of the ideas I have suggested will take patience and perseverance, others approach the theme of decorating with metallics in instantly accessible and novel ways.

Gilding is the art of affixing a thin coating of metal, in leaf or powdered form, to surfaces such as wood, gesso, stucco, paper, glass, metal or fabric. It can also refer to bronzing and lacquer work. It may be seen as an attempt to suggest that an object is made of solid gold, silver or copper, yet its decorative nature is more complex than this, since the innate quality of the gilded object remains – the flexibility of paper, the transparency of glass or the warmth of wood. The traditional methods of gilding have been in use since

antiquity, when the practice was often undertaken in secrecy, and the process has changed little over time.

This collection of ideas should be seen as an introduction to metallic finishes. My aim has been to open up new possibilities, using different materials to demonstrate a range of striking and unusual forms of decoration. The suggestions include easily achievable paint effects as well as touching on the more specialized techniques. My hope is that the easier 'pseudo' gilded finishes may lead you into a more all-encompassing involvement with the more challenging areas of real gilding and metal patination.

The traditional methods are complex, time-consuming and demanding, but richly rewarding. An appreciation of such skills is necessary in anyone interested in specialist decoration, as we must understand the real value of traditional skills in order to be confident about applying them to our modern environment in innovative, exciting and fresh ways.

Loose leaf, applied with the traditional water-gilding method, can then be burnished to a rich sheen.

Decorative mouldings treated with traditional gilding methods using a range of metal leaves and surfaces. The colour of the surface beneath the metal will have an effect on the colour of the finished article.

Alternative new products on the market can offer us a whole new language to use, but it is important to understand the traditional methods of preparation, application and patination to help to sustain good decoration. If we concentrate too exclusively on superficial methods of decorating for the sake of instant gratification, we stand to lose the durability and depth of the decorative language, which may result in a gap in our cultural history: the work we do will not last and the skills of the past will be lost as the technical range becomes temporary and uniform.

Any new decorative effect needs to be considered carefully, as outside influences on your personal taste can be subliminal: fads and fashions dictate ideas but in your own surroundings you may wish to use the suggestion of a new style while still integrating it with the old and familiar. There is current interest in using reflective surfaces and metals to give a sharper, more utilitarian feel to the environment, which is usually achieved by the use of stainless steel, aluminium and copper, but these materials can have an industrial feel which may not be quite what you are after. As a gentler alternative, I have suggested paint effects that offer a softer, more irregular finish.

I have aimed to show how unique, interesting interiors can be inspired by everyday materials: with some imagination you can obtain the look of the moment without incurring huge expense, while adding your own unique touch at the same time. Too many smooth, unyielding finishes can start to become hostile over time; creating your own handmade surfaces gives a more sensual, subtle variety to your

Examples of the range of colours available in metallic paints and metal leaf.

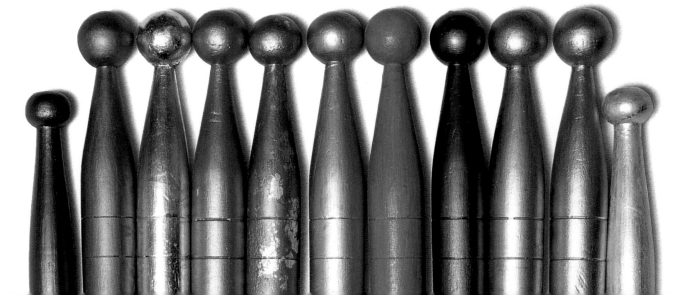

surroundings while suggesting the tangible qualities of the original material. The fact that such effects have the ability to age and change can be reassuring. Controlling and encouraging this ageing with various methods of distressing and patinating allows it to occur gracefully and beautifully, with the finesse of sympathetic detailing and finishing.

The calculated use of metallic effects can give you the opportunity to demonstrate wit, introduce elements of surprise and express your personality. An unassuming piece of furniture can be given a new sparkling character by applying bright, shimmering colour, suddenly turning it into a precious object with new inherent value. You can keep to the more restrained tones, colours and textures I have suggested, but it is fun to experiment occasionally, to add sparkle and an element of the exotic to your life. The creative process involved in deciding how and where to add metallic finishes can generate a sense of adventure in your own environment. It can be a catalyst for more innovative or dramatic changes and it can induce a sense of luxury and stimulation, even when the effects are created using the most mundane of materials.

Kerry Skinner

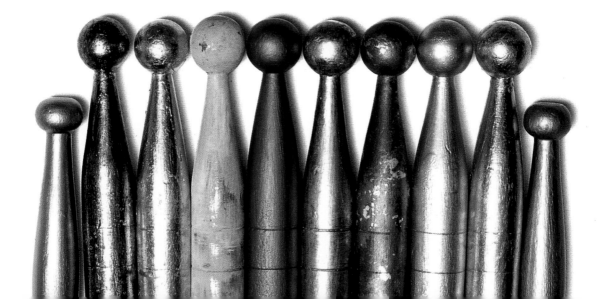

surfaces

introduction

A gilded panel carved from stucco rather than the traditional gesso is easier to create yet retains the warmth of the original.

This selection of decorative projects should be seen as an introduction to the application and use of metallic finishes. I hope you will be inspired to mix and match colours and techniques to find your own expressive language. The huge range of products on the market could start you on new adventures with decorative surfaces, contrasting matt and shine, subtle lustres and more gaudy and obvious glitters and spangles. I have included the techniques of water-, oil- and acrylic-size gilding, covering the principles I believe you should consider when tackling these skills. Other projects demonstrate some of the effects you can achieve using oil- and water-based metallic paints, metal and bronze powders and a variety of possible combinations.

Preparation of the underlying surface is extremely important, as the effects can easily crack, peel or not adhere properly if you have overlooked this stage. Do also follow the advice offered on applying protective finishes, as it would be such a disappointment to find your hard work suffering damage because it was completed in haste.

When you are planning to integrate a metallic finish into your home, recognize that you are not only introducing another light-reflecting surface but a new texture and, very importantly, a new colour. Silver can appear cold in an inappropriate setting, while gold can seem flashy and dominating in a neutral scheme.

Metallic finishes combine well with each other, as well as with natural textures, such as wood.

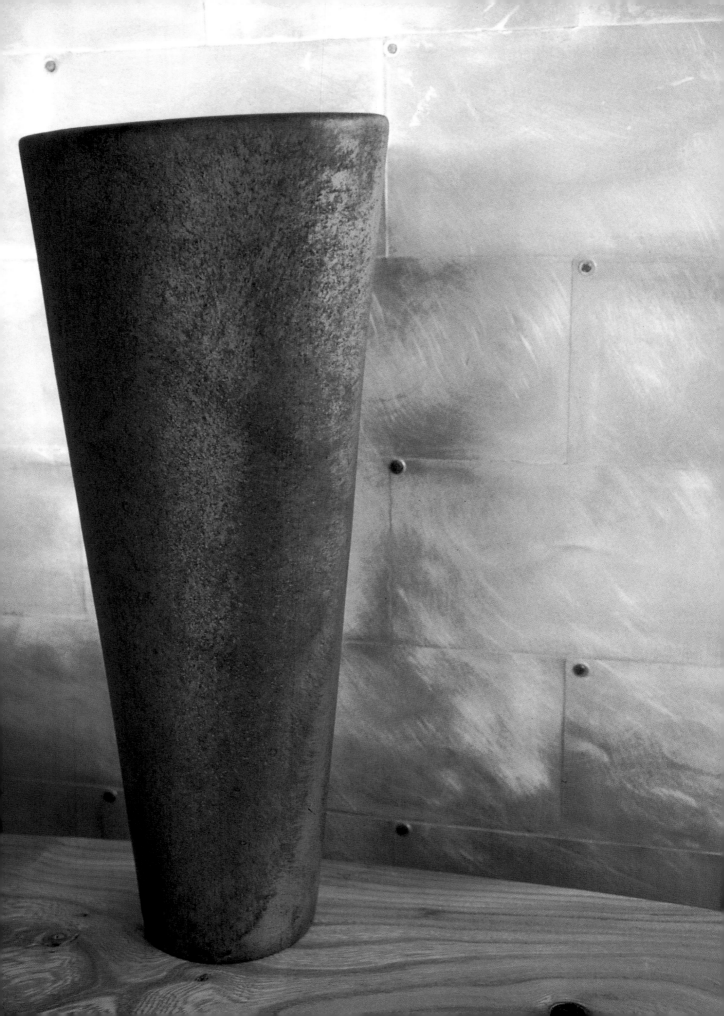

Although the reflective qualities of metallics suggest the introduction of extra light, the surfaces themselves can actually appear very dark. The level and quality of light will have a profound effect on all metallic finishes.

A metallic wall or floor will alter the mood and atmosphere of the total environment. In both natural and artificial light, the reflective surface will offer changes in colour and levels of intensity. Over a large area, the dramatic texture of a metallic effect may mean that the surface looks too emphatic and busy, and you may come to feel that you need something softer and more harmonious to live with on a daily basis. For this reason, you should always try out ideas on a sample board and place it in different locations, looking at it in both daylight and artificial light before beginning work. Decoration on a large scale can be a long process and needs a confident approach.

Despite these warnings, don't be afraid to jump in and try as many techniques as you can, as your experiments could provide the new aesthetic language you require to achieve a fascinating balance of colour, texture and style, transforming ordinary materials and bringing glamour to the most basic surfaces. The application of a metallic finish can be unusually illuminating, bringing vibrancy to a dull room or object as its new texture stimulates a sense of space and appreciation. It can add a different flavour to your home and a richness to the way you experience your environment.

The shine of metal is complemented by matt textures in this patinated wall effect.

Subtle effects can be achieved by washes of metallic paints, built up in layers and distressed.

faux-gold wall

This is one of the most luxurious, glamorous wall effects ever. I have used it as a background in hallways to display dark wood furniture, as a warm contrasting feature against blue walls, and as a foil to deep red fabrics and terracotta flooring. It warms and reflects light in the most spectacular way, and is an accessible introduction to some of the skills entailed in adding the gleam of gold, before moving on to more authentic, traditional techniques. While Dutch metal gilding does not having the radiance of water-gilding or the brilliance of oil-gilding, it is an affordable method of creating a luxurious expanse of gold. An underlying coat of red paint enhances the effect by imitating traditional red clay bole.

The reflective surface of this wall will have a constantly changing appearance, depending on the way the room is lit. To tone down its brilliance and add the character of age, the wall has been patinated using oil colours. If your overall scheme includes colours you wish to echo on the wall, add these in some areas and work the layers into each other as shown. The pattern made by the squares of leaf adds its own subtle geometry to the room, matching the simple lines of the fireplace and shelves. This understated design could be taken up in other parts of the room to unify the decorative scheme.

Gilding and patination on a large scale give the room a warm and beautiful focus, enhancing an unusual display of sculpture and other objects.

faux-gold wall

Focus on Technique

Dutch metal leaf can be applied using either acrylic or oil size. While oil size is more expensive and takes longer to dry, the finished surface is easier to distress. If time is limited use acrylic, but ensure that the wall is perfectly sound as acrylic size does not appear to dry as completely as oil, which can make it susceptible to peeling if the surface is not prepared carefully. The addition of shellac and thin layers of oil paint give additional protection against surface damage, as well as disguising any imperfections in the wall.

Materials and Equipment

interior filler
fine wet-and-dry sandpaper
matt emulsion paint in deep red
paintbrushes
paint kettles
tape measure
chalk line
spirit level
steel rule
pencil
12-hour or acrylic size
transfer Dutch metal leaf in gold
soft lint-free cloth
soft brush
jam jar
clear shellac
wire wool
artist's oil paints: burnt umber, Payne's grey and
    burnt sienna
white spirit
cellulose decorator's sponge
clear beeswax (optional)

Preparation

Fill any holes, sand the wall thoroughly and remove any dust. Make sure the surface is perfectly sound and dry.

1 Brush on two coats of deep red matt emulsion paint in imitation of red clay bole. The brush strokes should be varied in direction to ensure an even coverage. When the paint is dry give the wall a careful light sanding and retouch where necessary.

4 Wait until the size feels tacky, then begin to apply the transfer metal leaf. Place the leaf on the wall square by square, rubbing the back of each sheet with your hand or a pad of soft cloth, then removing the backing paper.

2 Measure the wall and mark the centre to establish the position of the squares. Use a chalk line and spirit level to divide the wall into appropriately sized squares (the squares of leaf should overlap slightly). Use a steel rule and pencil to give more defined lines, as the chalk will brush off when you size.

3 Apply the size over the whole surface to be gilded. Re-coat any areas that appear too matt as this indicates that the size has been absorbed into the painted surface and will not be receptive to the metal leaf. If you are using 12-hour size, you will need to apply it the night before you gild.

5 When you have completely covered the area, brush off the loose leaf gently using a soft brush. Collect the flakes of gold in a jam jar. You can re-size and repair any patches which have not held the metal leaf, using the brushed-off flakes.

6 Apply a coat of clear shellac and leave to dry. This will protect the leaf and prevent it from tarnishing, and provide a surface to take the oil paint.

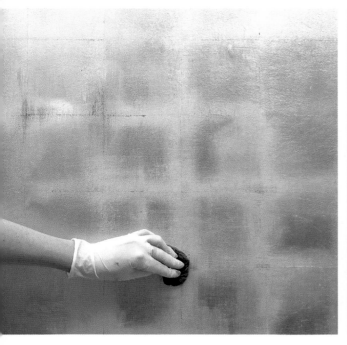

7 The gold can now be distressed with wire wool to bring out the base colour and create some toning. This slight abrasion will help to key the surface for the layers of oil paint.

8 Dilute the oil paints with white spirit and wash them lightly over parts of the surface. Allow the colours to run down the wall but control the process by sponging off excess paint.

9 Leave the paint to dry for a while, then use a wide brush to spatter the surface with white spirit. As it begins to dry, the paint can be softened with a sponge or soft cloth, dabbed off and wiped thin.

10 Repeat these processes until you are happy with the effect. You can also work back into the wall with wire wool when the paint is completely dry. Finish off with another coat of shellac and/or beeswax for extra protection.

metallic-effect floor tiles

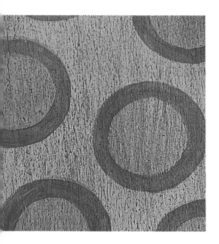

Floors tend to be kept neutral in most modern schemes, but this is an adventurous departure from the norm, and an idea that is easy to adapt to suit your own colour scheme. The tiles are made of plywood, which will not shrink or warp and can be cut at a local woodyard to any size that suits the dimensions of your floor, though this random, multi-coloured design works best if the individual squares are fairly large. Try to keep the patterns as simple as possible to ensure the tiles do not jar with each other and the overall design does not become too distracting. The huge range of metallic colours available gives you a wide spectrum to work with. As the colours are built up thinly and always lightly sanded between coats, you can achieve subtle depths of textural shading.

The tiles should be glued down on a level floor using contact adhesive, and the gaps can be grouted if you wish, as with any other tiles. The finish is robust and practical, the surface is easy to clean and the colours should not fade much with age. The protective varnish can be lightly sanded and recoated to the density you prefer. Use a gloss varnish if you want a shinier look. As an alternative, treat the tiles with a layer of wax buffed up to give a smooth sheen.

A random design of patterned, painted tiles is unified by the use of simple geometric designs and a subtle range of metallic colours. It brings a new focus to the room.

metallic-effect floor tiles

Focus on Technique

The secret to achieving a good finish is to sand between layers and build up the colours in thin coats of paint: this may seem laborious but it will ensure the decoration is still evident however much everyday use may wear away the top layers. If you compromise on this process the paint may chip unattractively rather than age gracefully.

Materials and Equipment

plywood squares
fine wet-and-dry sandpaper
white spirit
soft lint-free cloths
oil-based metal primer: black and red oxide
paintbrushes
oil-based metallic paints: silver, gold and copper
paint kettles
masking tape
round templates
pencil
acrylic metallic paints in a variety of colours
cellulose decorator's sponges
straight edge
eggshell oil-based varnish

Preparation

Lightly sand the top surface and edges of each tile. Wipe over with white spirit to remove the dust. If you are planning a design with a regular pattern, divide the wooden tiles into piles to be painted in the appropriate base colours. Bear in mind that the final coat of varnish will darken the colours considerably.

1

Paint each tile with oil-based primer, making sure the paint is even and all the edges are covered. Both sides of the tiles should be primed to prevent any warping.

2

The primer will dry quickly and may be ready to repaint the same day. Sand the tiles before applying the next layer of metallic paint. This will help to key the surface and keep it even.

3

Stir the metallic oil paints well as directed and apply the base colours using a broad brush. Some paints may be thinner than others and you may need to apply more coats to get a solid finish. Always leave to dry thoroughly and sand lightly between coats.

4

When you are happy with the base colour and have sanded the surface again, you can start to apply the decorative shapes and patterns. Keep the designs simple. Use masking tape to make simple stripes and pot lids or saucers for circles. You can rework the base colours to break up the squares with a series of geometric shapes.

5

Build up thin layers of metallic acrylic paint using a damp sponge. The acrylic paint will hold well if the surface of the oil-based paint has been keyed with light sanding. If you mask out areas that are painted already you can keep washing over more colours.

6

When the paint is dry, remove any masking tape and lightly sand again.

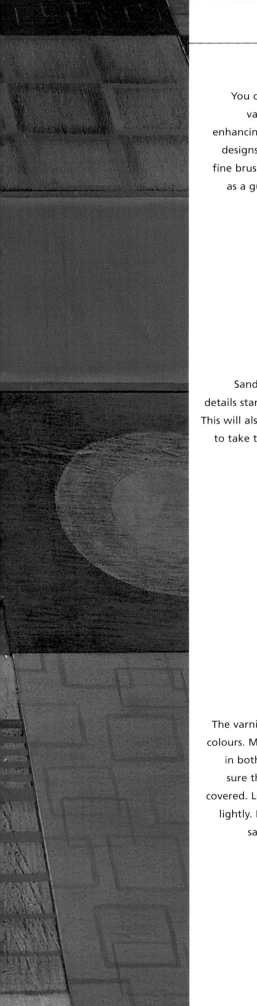

7

You can now add details in various metallic colours, enhancing and contrasting the designs with outlines using a fine brush. Use a straight edge as a guide for straight lines.

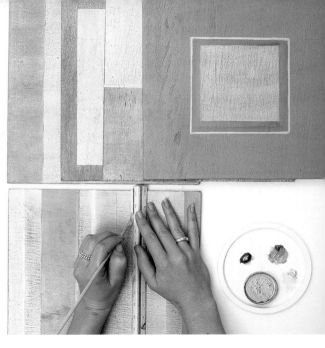

8

Sand again to prevent the details standing out too sharply. This will also prepare the surface to take the protective varnish.

9

The varnish will deepen all the colours. Make the brush strokes in both directions and make sure that the edges are also covered. Leave to dry then sand lightly. Re-coat at least twice, sanding between coats.

aluminium wall-cladding

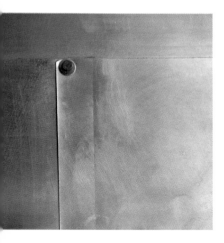

This is one of my favourite projects, as the technique is simple but has maximum impact. Its inspiration was the titanium cladding on the Guggenheim Museum in Bilbao, Spain, whose reflective plates follow every plane of the extraordinary building. Seeing it prompted me to try many experiments with aluminium foil and thin sheeting to find a simple, reasonably priced method of emulating it in a domestic context. The utilitarian appearance of the panelling suggests it might be most suitable for use in a kitchen, but it is well worth considering the effect in other living areas such as a dining or sitting room, since the cladding forms a wonderful contrasting background for luxurious upholstery fabrics and responds beautifully to soft lighting or candles.

The hard reflective appearance of metal panels can sharpen the look of an area and give it a modern industrial feel, but the slight irregularities of these small-scale aluminium plates create a more interesting texture which invites touch. The cladding is made of recycled aluminium in the form of printers' old lithography plates. As a result, the surface has a muted glow and a deeper tone than would be possible if new aluminium had been used, giving the wall a satisfying, lived-in look. The plates are glued to the wall, but the washer and tack detail gives a more secure fixing and adds the finishing touch to the design.

Traces of ink and colour remain from the previous life of this recycled aluminium, helping to create an interesting surface which has been enhanced by polishing with abrasive wire wool.

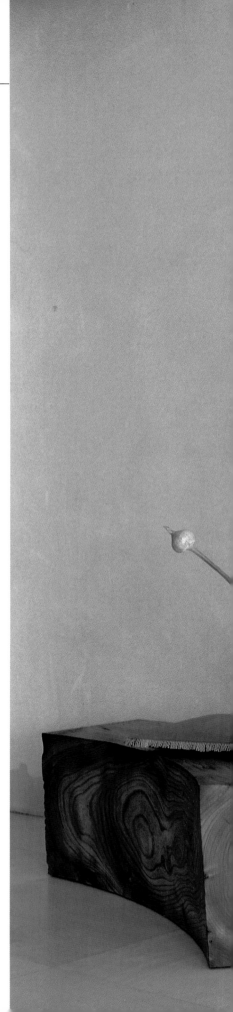

aluminium wall-cladding

Focus on Technique

This easy and affordable technique can be achieved by anyone with some basic skills in DIY. Overlap the plates to keep the appearance neat and make fixing firmer: mark the overlaps with a pencil to help with alignment. If the panelling is to be attached to a plaster wall rather than hardboard, the wall will have to be drilled at each fixing point and the plates attached using small screws in each corner rather than tacks.

Materials and Equipment

hardboard-covered room divider
tape measure
recycled aluminium lithography plates
cutting mat
steel rule
craft knife
pencil
metal file
contact adhesive
glue spreader
wire wool
methylated spirit
soft lint-free cloth
bradawl
small washers
tacks
hammer

Preparation

Contact a local printer to request used lithography plates. These are made in different gauges so you will need to ask for 0.3mm sheeting, which can be cut with a knife or scissors. Get enough to allow for some wastage, as the plates will have bent edges and some damage from being attached to the press. The board or wall surface must be as smooth and flat as possible.

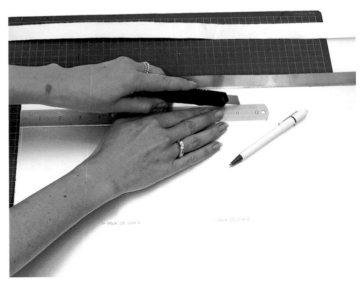

1 Measure the area to be covered and decide on the size of each plate. Allow an extra 1cm/½in on each edge for overlap. To cover a free-standing room divider, allow an extra section at the end of each horizontal band to fold over the edges. Trim off the bent edges, then mark up and cut out the plates.

4 Position the plates in the second row so that the joins are midway between those of the first, and overlap the first row by 1cm/½in. For the third and subsequent rows, use a ruler to align the joins in alternate rows.

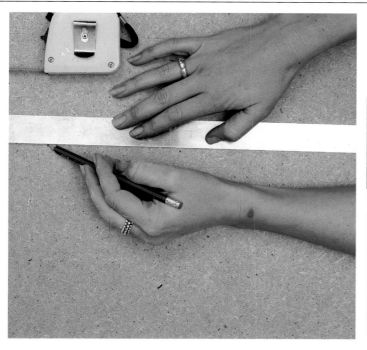

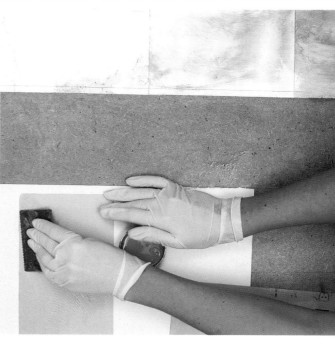

2 Measure and mark a series of horizontal lines across the hardboard to use as guidelines for placing the rows of plates. A few discrepancies will occur, and will add to the character of the panelling, but use the lines to keep the rows as straight as possible.

3 File the edges of each individual plate, slightly rounding the corners. Glue the plates to the panel, beginning at the top or bottom and working from one end to the other of the first row. Spread contact adhesive thinly on both surfaces and allow a few minutes' drying time before positioning each plate.

5 When the whole surface is covered, clean the metal with wire wool and methylated spirit to remove pencil marks and traces of printing ink. Rub in a regular circular motion to give the metal a subtle texture, then wipe over with a clean cloth and methylated spirit to remove any surface dirt.

6 Make a small hole using a bradawl at each overlapping corner, then place a small washer over each hole and hammer a tack into the panel.

stucco panels

This uncomplicated juxtaposition of coloured stucco and gold leaf produces a harmony of textures and colours, combining natural materials in a simple, graphic decorative style. The minimal design allows you to enjoy the integrity of the materials with no distracting detailing.

The warm red stucco has a velvety surface reminiscent of the red clay bole used in traditional gilding. It acts as a richly textured and coloured border for the gold, which is laid in a central panel cut into the stucco surface. In practical terms, stucco plaster is a suitable substitute for a gesso base, as it forms a powdery, smooth foundation for the application of the leaf which is almost as sensitive to work with as traditional gesso. The sheen of the polished and waxed plaster makes you want to touch it – the surface actually has a warmth and smoothness which is very different to the colder, harder feel of the gold. In both colour and texture the materials are sympathetic and combine beautifully.

It is best to be on the safe side and make sure the panels are not displayed too close to heat, sunlight or moisture, although the wax finish will act as a protective barrier.

Two matching panels positioned symmetrically in this hallway create a touch of abstract drama.

stucco panels

Focus on Technique

Wooden board has been used for this panel, but
stucco can also be applied to a wall if it is very
smoothly primed. All-purpose filler is applied to the
board in imitation of traditional gesso. If you are
experienced in working with gesso, you may wish to
use the real thing instead. The metal leaf can be real
gold or Dutch metal: the latter will require a coat of
varnish or shellac. The size used can be rabbit-skin, oil
or acrylic. The first two offer a better finish for the
wire wool distressing, as acrylic is more likely to resist
and may peel over time.

Materials and Equipment

wooden board
white acrylic primer or paint
all-purpose filler
paint kettle
paintbrushes
fine wet-and-dry sandpaper
pencil and steel rule
metal scraper
cellulose decorator's sponge
acrylic paint in burnt sienna
lime-compatible pigments: terracotta and red
jars and flat containers
ready-mixed white stucco plaster
sealed boards for mixing
filling knives
scrap paper
soft lint-free cloths
rabbit-skin, oil or acrylic size
transfer Dutch metal or real gold leaf
soft brush
wire wool
clear beeswax

Preparation

Prepare the board by painting it with white acrylic
primer or paint, to which you have added all-purpose
filler. Apply at least eight coats, sanding between
each, to build up enough depth to cut out the central
panel. Mark out the central area and cut into the
prepared imitation gesso, using a metal scraper to
create the lower level for the gilding. Do not worry if
you make mistakes or cut too deeply as the surface is
easy to repair. Lightly sand the relief edges.

1 Using a damp sponge, wash two thin coats of dilute
burnt sienna acrylic paint over the surface. Dilute
each pigment with a little water, then mix into a
small amount of plaster in a flat container (transfer it
to a board to mix it properly). Paint a sample of each
colour on to paper to check the colour when dry.

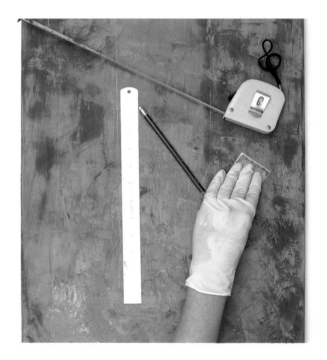

4 Leave the stucco to dry then use a filling knife to
polish it. With the blade flat, work over the plaster in
all directions, bringing up a soft sheen. You may
need to define the inner shape again: if necessary
lightly scrape away some of the stucco then polish
with a soft cloth to prevent it being too porous.

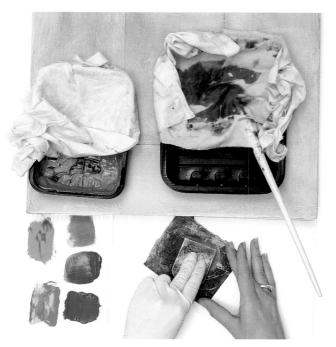

2 Lay a damp cloth over the plasters to keep from drying out. The plaster is applied with filling knives, which will need to be prepared with bevelled edges. Dampen some wet-and-dry paper and lay it on a flat surface. Hold each blade at a shallow angle and rub the edge in a circular motion. Smooth the corners.

3 Start with the light plaster and use a filling knife to pull thinly across the surface. Change direction regularly and apply at least four coats. Use a smaller knife to add deeper colours. If the plaster is too thick it may crack. Smooth the edges with your fingers. Repeat for the central area, with thinner layers.

5 Size the central panel, re-coating if too much of the size is absorbed. When the size is tacky apply the transfer leaf, overlapping the sheets slightly. Gently rub the back of the paper before lifting it off.

6 Dust off the excess gold with a soft brush. If the size is dry enough you can distress the gold slightly with wire wool. The whole surface can be protected with a layer of clear beeswax. Buff up with a soft cloth to leave a protective sheen.

metallic-patina wall

This is one version of a paint effect which can be used on any surface and can combine as many colours as your imagination allows. The interplay between the shiny reflective metallics and the matt paint gives a wealth of interesting layered textures, which is echoed in the contrast of warm and cold colours. At its best this effect can suggest the dappled shimmer of light on water, recalling the impressionism of Monet. Generally, it is a bold way to combine extraordinary colours and paints in a never-ending textural experiment, the results of which will be unique.

Try out the technique on a large-scale sample board first, keeping the colours similar in tone. Once you feel confident with dry brushing you can add as many layers as you wish. You will find other examples of patinas created in this way among the colour swatches at the end of the book, but you may prefer to study the effects that occur when real metals and alloys are subjected to ageing and chemical distressing, and experiment with replicating these in paint. For this project, the effect has been achieved using matt emulsion, but other matt paints such as blackboard paint, metal primer and flat oil paint can also be used. You can also achieve some highly original effects by working over textured backgrounds and lightly sanding between colours.

The interesting, varied patination of weathered metal can be reproduced by adding light touches of matt colour to a gold-painted wall.

metallic-patina wall

Focus on Technique

This is an example of dry brushing: the paint is brushed on in small amounts, without loading the brush too much. It takes some practice to keep your brush strokes short and regular, and to achieve a nice balance of colours. You need a feather touch and to be brave enough to start again if the colours become muddy. Leave the paint to dry thoroughly between each coat to avoid any smudging.

1 Dilute burnt sienna acrylic about 1:2 with water and use a sponge to wash it on to the wall in a series of cloudy circular layers. Leave to dry, then repeat until the required density is reached.

Materials and Equipment

matt emulsion paints: off-white, aqua blue and white
paint roller and tray
artist's acrylic paints: burnt sienna, rich gold,
   dark gold, lemon gold and light gold
paint kettles
cellulose decorator's sponge
paintbrushes
matt acrylic glaze (optional)
fine wet-and-dry sandpaper
soft lint-free cloth
clear beeswax

Preparation

Apply two coats of off-white emulsion paint to the prepared wall.

4 Mix some aqua blue emulsion 2:1 with white and dilute it slightly with water (you could also add a little matt acrylic glaze to increase the transparency). Apply to the wall using the same dry brush technique.

2 Build up a series of layers of different golds, starting with the lightest. The paint should be applied lightly with a dry brush, leaving some of the base colour showing. Brush strokes should be short, both vertical and horizontal.

3 Allow the paint to dry then apply a top coat of the lightest gold in more solid vertical strokes, filling in any areas that appear empty or too busy.

5 Apply the deeper aqua colour, also diluted, in the same way, concentrating it in particular areas rather than overall. The surface should begin to take on a dappled appearance, as if light is flickering across it.

6 Now re-work the colours, adding more light and dark golds until you achieve the right depth of colour and texture, but without making the effect too busy. When dry, lightly sand off any texture that has built up before giving the wall a protective layer of wax.

chequered silver wall

This is an unusual decoration with a relaxed, informal feel, for either a whole room or a feature wall such as a chimney breast. The basic square pattern is offset by an assortment of different shades of silver, with randomly distributed squares of metal leaf. The interest lies in the play of hard and soft, light and dark, with the brighter, harder-looking metal highlighting the more softly textured painted squares. The different lustres of the various silver colours have been brought together by gently distressing the whole wall with wire wool: as with many metallic finishes, this one becomes easier on the eye when the gaudy shine of new paint or metal leaf has been worn in slightly.

The lilac base colour is revealed occasionally, warming up the cooler silvers to give a subtle depth and richness. It also helps to balance the wall with the colour scheme used for the rest of the room, which is a combination of brown, grey, lilac and plum with sharper accents of silver. Rather than relying only on applied colour, this wall demonstrates a contemporary interest in texture as a way of bringing interest to interior decoration.

The wall will be greatly affected by varying light sources throughout the day and the year. Direct light will reflect off the harder metal of the leaf, while in soft light the effect will be a slight shimmer.

chequered silver wall

Focus on Technique

You can adapt this idea to any scale or surface if it is prepared properly. It uses very few materials and needs only basic measuring and painting skills. The aluminium leaf used will not tarnish and so therefore need not be protected with varnish, but you could add lustre by waxing the surface.

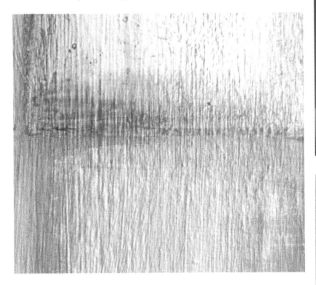

Materials and Equipment

matt emulsion paint in lilac

paintbrushes

paint kettles

wet-and-dry sandpaper

acrylic paint in silver

tape measure

chalk line and spirit level

pencil

steel rule

stencil card

cutting mat

craft knife

selection of artist's acrylic or oil paints in silver,
    or silver powders and various binders such as
    PVA glue, sanding sealer and wallpaper paste

acrylic size

transfer aluminium leaf

soft lint-free cloths

soft brush

jam jar

wire wool

clear beeswax

Preparation

Prepare the wall by filling any holes, sand the surface and wipe down to remove dust.

1

Paint the wall with lilac matt emulsion and allow to dry. Sand lightly, then apply a quick, dry-brushed coat of dilute acrylic silver paint. Start at the top of the wall and work down, using light, straight, regular brush strokes. Leave some of the base colour showing through.

4

Paint the remaining squares using vertical brush strokes. You could use a different silver paint for added interest. If you have silver powders, mix them with various binders to create different hues and finishes. Leave the remaining squares to dry.

2

When the wall is dry, mark out the squares, which should be no larger than the size of the aluminium leaf. On a large wall, use a chalk line to mark the horizontal and vertical lines, and check them with a spirit level.

5

Paint various random squares with acrylic size. Use a small artist's brush to paint a crisp edge around each square, then fill in with a larger brush. When the size is tacky, apply the transfer leaf and rub over the backing paper with your hand or a pad of soft cloth before removing it. Dust off the excess leaf with a soft brush and save the flakes in a jam jar.

3

Draw and cut some stencils to the size of the marked squares. You will need several as the card will distort with repeated use. Cut at least one stencil with only three sides to allow you to work up to the edges of the wall. Apply silver paint horizontally in alternate squares (you do not need to fill the whole shape). Leave to dry.

6

To tone down the aluminium you can lightly distress it with wire wool. Do this carefully in case the size begins to peel. Work along the edges of the squares with the wire wool, as darker edges will create a hint of relief. Protect the aluminium leaf with a layer of beeswax.

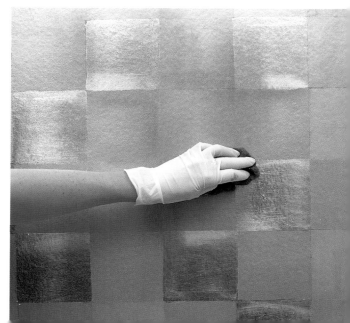

water-gilded panel

This panel can be adapted to suit the size of your environment and your budget – the same techniques and principles apply no matter what size area you choose to cover. I wanted to emphasize the intrinsic qualities of the metal leaf, taking advantage of the regular-sized squares and incorporating them into a discreet surface pattern. The edges of the leaf do not overlap in places, allowing the colour of the bole underneath to show through. The central panel was intensified by double-gilding and burnishing with a traditional gilder's agate burnisher. This brought out the shine, creating a subtle contrast of textures with the surrounding area, which was left unburnished, while some squares were distressed with wire wool to heighten the textural contrasts.

The panel is a patchwork of different types of metal leaf. Some squares were brushed with parchment size, some were burnished, some were left in their natural state. Experiment with different combinations of leaf, highlighting specific areas with a burnishing tool. Use the effect to cover an entire wall, a tiny panel or a cupboard door – it will bring a lustrous glow to any room.

Squares of gold leaf were applied to a panel, with some areas burnished to a shimmering sheen. The result is a modern work of art that evokes the gold-leaf backgrounds of Russian icons.

water-gilded panel

Focus on Technique

This panel is an experimental piece to practise water-gilding and to try out different colours and methods of using gold leaf. Instructions for preparing the size, gesso and bole can be found in the Techniques section at the back of the book. The preparation of the gesso base is crucial, and it is important to use the same mix for all the layers. Red bole, mixed with size, will provide colour enrichment and limit the absorption of the size used in applying the gold leaf. It is important to work methodically when gilding, as any size not covered will show as a stain and create a matt surface which is less easy to burnish.

Materials and Equipment

softwood battens for frame
saw
wood glue
hammer and nails
hardboard
all-purpose filler
fine wet-and-dry sandpaper
fine linen
rabbit-skin size
home-made gesso (see Techniques)
saucepans and bowls
hog's hair brushes
soft lint-free cloths
flat metal scraper
red bole (see Techniques)
loose gold leaf
gilder's tip
petroleum jelly (optional)
gilder's cushion
gilder's knife
gilder's mop
set square
fine wire wool
steel rule
clear beeswax

Preparation

Construct a frame from lengths of softwood and attach a piece of smooth-faced hardboard. Fill and sand the board, then soak fine linen in size and apply it to the corners of the frame to prevent any further movement as this would dislodge the gesso. Treat the board with a coat of dilute size to prepare for the gesso.

1

Make up the gesso following the instructions at the back of the book, and apply it to the board using a hog's hair brush, brushing in well in different directions. Apply at least eight coats, adding each when the previous one is matt but not completely dry.

2

For the smoothest possible surface, sand lightly with fine wet-and-dry paper. Wet the paper and keep a layer of water between it and the gesso. Wipe the surface with a wet cloth to create a 'slurry' of gesso which will fill in any hollows. Leave to dry overnight, then use a flat metal scraper to re-cut the surface: hold this at an angle and pull diagonally in one direction, then the other. The gesso can be wet-polished again, then left to dry.

3

Apply a good coat of red bole, brushing in alternate directions to ensure an even layer. Keep the bowl of clay in a pan of warm water while you work. Leave to dry overnight.

4

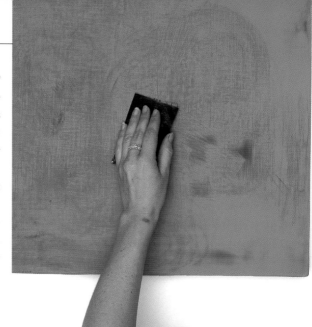

Polish up the bole with fine wet-and-dry paper. (Two pieces of paper can be rubbed together first to give a smoother abrasive surface.) Work in a regular circular motion and dust off the surface with a soft brush and cloth. You may notice some colour difference if the surface is not smooth enough: apply another coat of bole if the irregularities are too obvious, leave to dry, then sand again.

5

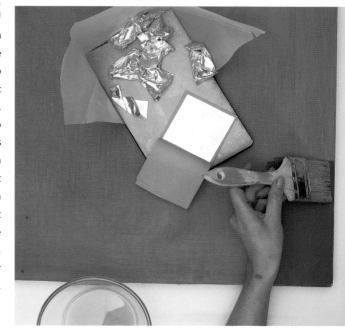

You are now ready to begin gilding. Raise the panel at one end to give a slight incline, so any excess size-water will not run over the newly laid gold. You will need to work fast, so have the gold leaf and gilder's tip ready, and the diluted size in a bowl near at hand. Do not flood the bole with too much size-water or the gold will not apply evenly. Apply the size with a soft bristle brush, covering an area slightly larger than a leaf of gold.

6

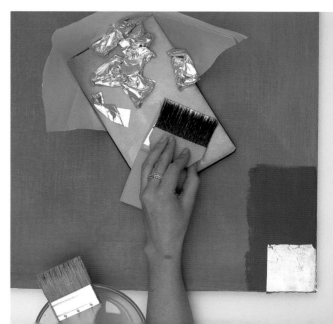

The gold does not need to be cut for this panel, so you can pick up the leaves straight from the book. It is worth practising cutting and blowing the gold flat on the cushion as you may need small pieces for 'faulting' or patching up areas. Wipe the gilder's tip across your skin or use a little petroleum jelly to help hold the gold in place. Touch the tip to the sheet and raise it carefully, avoiding creating air movement.

7

The leaf will be pulled off the tip by capillary attraction; the movement to lay it down must be confident and smooth. Start by touching the gold to the surface with the tip almost parallel. If the sheet folds or breaks you should remove it with a damp brush and start again for a perfect finish. If you are working fast, the area you have sized already may have a film of size ready to take another sheet. If not, re-wet the bole before picking up the next piece. Lay the next leaf so that it overlaps the previous one. This will allow for any size-water seepage, which would stain the surface.

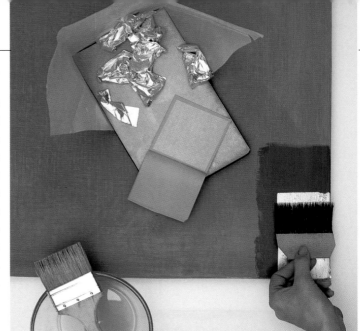

8

As the size begins to dry, use the gilder's mop to tamp down the sheets to ensure that bubbles of air or water are patted out. Try to work with the brush held at 90° to avoid tearing the leaf.

9

To create a fairly solid gilded surface for burnishing you can apply a second layer of leaf, but do not touch the surface, as the grease from your hands will make it too resistant. 'Double-gilding' must be done carefully to avoid disturbing the first layer. Use less size, brush it over only once and overlap the leaf as before. Some repairs can be made if you feel the bole is appearing too obviously. If you have many water stains you may be able to 'fault' these with a warm breath over the stain and the quick application of a piece of leaf.

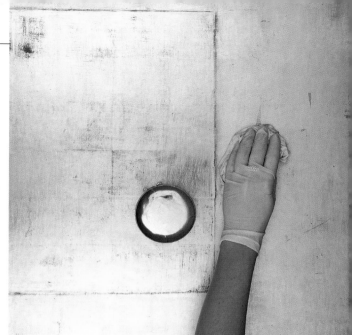

10

Once you are happy with the gilding you can experiment with methods of ageing, distressing and burnishing (see Techniques). To define the double-gilded 'frame' and central panel, use fine wire wool wiped along a straight edge to rub through and bring up the bole colour. The easiest and most subtle finish is achieved by an application of beeswax, polished on and buffed up with a soft cloth.

furniture

introduction

The MDF surface of a curved desk has been transformed with copper leaf.

Metal leaf and powders, metallic paint, paper, foil and copper wire are all used in the following projects to create a range of new surfaces and textures for what could loosely be called interior furniture. As with all effects the results will vary, but the techniques described can be used as a basis for your own experiments. As always, the initial preparation of the surface is crucial for a successful result, as all metallic finishes need to adhere well if they are to last.

All the objects shown are designed to be functional, so the finishes need to be protected by layers of lacquer, varnish or wax. This will not stop them wearing altogether, but any wear and tear should occur in an agreeable way, demonstrating the passage of time and regular use in similar style to the surface of an item made of a natural material such as wood, stone or real metal. Most of the same principles apply to finishes on objects designed to be used out of doors, and it is well worth trying metallics in this context: the use of varnishes appropriate for exterior use will enable you to protect the finishes against mild conditions in the garden.

The decorative use of gilding and other metallic effects on furniture has a long history. Mesopotamian inventories over 5,000 years old describe gilded furniture, and the technique of decorating wood with gold leaf or thin gold sheathing was used by the ancient Egyptians – an early example of gilded

The foliated capital of a plaster column is decorated with silver acrylic paint. This is easier to apply than silver leaf, yet still transforms the original piece.

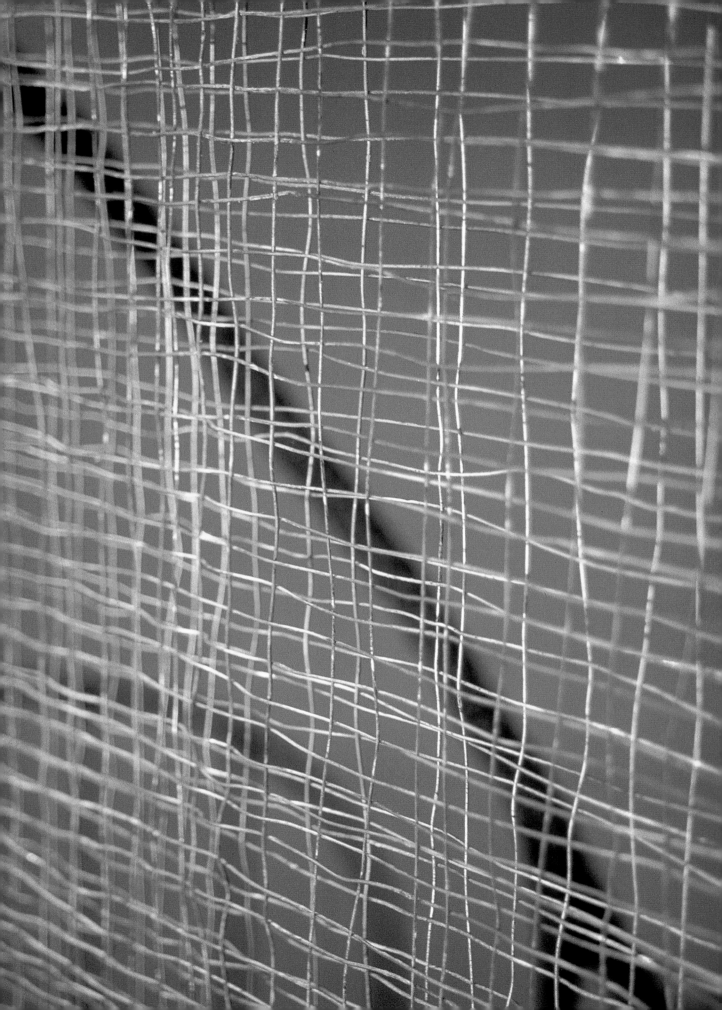

furniture found in a royal tomb dates from about 2600 BC. By the Hellenistic period, Egyptian gilders were using both water- and oil-gilding, and these techniques passed into the European tradition. In the 16th and 17th centuries, Chinese craftsmen produced extraordinary decorative items in lacquer work, often embellished with metallic powders and gilding. This technique spread to Japan, and then Europe, where it was imitated using the method known as Japanning, which involved gilding of great delicacy and detail.

Combine different metallic effects: here a dresser covered in metallic paper is positioned in front of an abstract panel decorated with metal leaf.

I am not suggesting that these pieces of furniture are of this nature – rather the opposite. I have sometimes suggested a quite irreverent use of materials, which has resulted in projects that are fun to achieve and do not require the skill of a master craftsman. My main aim has been to introduce ideas and techniques which are a starting point for more personal experiments, in view of the increasing popularity of metallic finishes within a decorative scheme. There is a new interest in the textures of metallics and the balance of smooth and rough, matt and shine in contemporary interiors.

Applied metallic decoration can transform any object to suggest weight, resistance and solidity. The range of options clearly demonstrates the flexibility of metallic effects: in each of the projects presented here the object has been treated to an inexpensive yet durable face-lift, to create an original piece of decorative furniture. A shiny, glamorous finish can give a tired piece of furniture a new lease of life and create an attractive, shimmering focal point in a room.

Patinated metal wire woven to create a screen will glitter as the natural light source changes.

copper-leaf curved desk

The shape of this desk demonstrates a departure in design which has been made possible by a change in emphasis in the modern working environment. With the down-sizing of computers and the advent (in theory, at least) of the paperless society it is becoming increasingly feasible to work in a smaller area, with concealed storage space for printers, scanners and other equipment. This is especially relevant when your workplace is also your home. There is no reason why functional furniture should not contribute decoratively to your surroundings. The large rectangular work desk can be a thing of the past, and you can experiment with more organic shapes, which fit sympathetically into a room, are easier to move around and more fun to decorate.

This desk is constructed from MDF with a curved plywood side. The top has been given a smooth, hard-wearing finish with a few coats of copper spray lacquer and the side has been transformed with copper leaf. This makes it look strong and stable, while the metallic sheen catching the light emphasizes its smooth contours. The uneven patina of the chemically treated copper leaf has a worn-in look. Its restrained tones give an unusual depth of texture which is visually stimulating while working in harmony with its surroundings. The aesthetic quality of industrial materials is often best realized when contrasted with softer, more luxurious materials.

The desk has been given a texture and colour that helps it fit in with its environment while introducing the suggestion of weight and modern styling.

copper-leaf curved desk

Focus on Technique

The curved side of the desk has been covered in copper leaf, which is thicker than other leaf so can be used loose and applied by hand. Cover your fingers with whiting before handling the leaf so that they do not transfer grease to the metal, which would prevent it adhering to the size.

Materials and Equipment

wooden desk
fine wet-and-dry sandpaper
acrylic primer
paintbrushes
flat oil paint in terracotta
matt emulsion paint in terracotta
tape measure
steel rule
pencil
acrylic size
pounce bag with whiting
loose copper leaf
soft brush
jam jar
copper spray paint
verdigris patinating fluid
cellulose decorator's sponge
clear shellac

Preparation

Sand and prime the desk, then sand again. Paint the desk top with flat oil paint in terracotta, and the base with matt emulsion paint. Leave to dry.

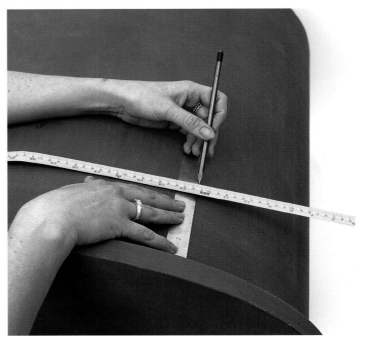

1 Using a tape measure, steel rule and pencil, mark the side of the desk with guidelines for positioning the copper leaf. Make the pencil squares slightly smaller than the copper, so that the leaves overlap.

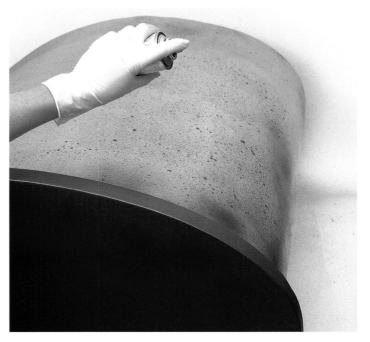

4 Spray the desk top with copper paint, repeating as necessary. For extra interest add some spray paint to the gilded copper (this will also be affected by the patination fluid). If you spray without shaking the can you can create a spotting effect. Leave to dry.

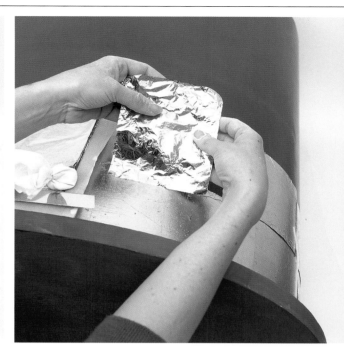

2 Brush acrylic size over the desk side, using regular brush strokes and smoothing out the size so that there is not too much build-up of texture. Work in sections to make sure that you cover the entire surface. Leave until tacky.

3 Cover your hands in whiting before handling the copper. Starting at the top, apply the leaf from one end of the first row to the other, overlapping the squares. Continue until the side is completely covered, then dust off any loose leaf with a soft brush and save the flakes in a jam jar.

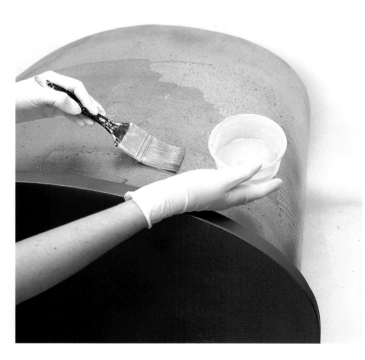

5 Apply the patinating fluid over the copper leaf using a soft brush. (If you wish to keep the patina subtle dilute the fluid slightly with water.) Keep the fluid moving until the colour begins to change.

6 As soon as you see the colour change, sponge off the fluid with water. Leave to dry, repeating if you wish to achieve further coloration. For a more definite verdigris finish leave the fluid on to dry. When totally dry, rub off the powder to expose the copper. Seal the surface with clear shellac to prevent tarnishing.

moroccan-style shutters

These shutters have been given a copper verdigris finish to add interest and weight to what could appear a flimsy window treatment. The addition of random texture and colour gives the frame an appearance of aged metal. The subtlety of the finish makes the effect equally interesting close up, as the simple design allows you to concentrate on the patina.

The finish appears more complicated to create than it actually is. After some initial experiments on sample boards, it becomes quite easy to control the random nature of the effect. Some paint companies offer 'patinating' fluids in blue or green that can be mixed to achieve a multi-coloured finish. The warmth of the copper-coloured surround and the cool tones of the blue-green patina create a harmonious and interesting combination.

This decoration can be applied to almost any surface but must always be sealed if you wish to preserve the colour as planned; if moisture can get to the surface, the copper will continue to change colour over time.

These fretwork-panelled shutters are greatly enhanced by the metallic patina. The subtle copper glow creates an impression of solidity that the simple MDF shutters would not normally have. The light filtering through the panels complements the glittering effect.

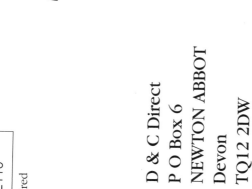

D & C Direct
P O Box 6
NEWTON ABBOT
Devon
TQ12 2DW

We'd like to hear from you...

Thank you for choosing this book. We'd like to hear from you because your comments will help us create the best and most innovative books possible. As a thank you for completing this form and helping us with our publishing research, we'll enter you in our quarterly free book give-away. Just complete and post this card and if you're a winner, we'll send you a free book in one of the subject areas in which you've expressed an interest. We'll also send you information about our new and forthcoming titles.

Title purchased: _____

Comments: _____

I am especially interested in the following subjects:

- [ ] Fine Art
- [ ] Practical Art
- [ ] Crafts
- [ ] Needlecrafts
- [ ] Miniatures/Dolls' Houses
- [ ] Woodworking
- [ ] Gardening
- [ ] Equestrian
- [ ] Children's Books
- [ ] Puzzles/Games

- [ ] Home Decorating
- [ ] Cookery
- [ ] Health/Complementary Medicine
- [ ] Personal Development
- [ ] Spirituality
- [ ] Photography
- [ ] Walking
- [ ] Country

- [ ] 0-3
- [ ] 3-5
- [ ] 5-7
- [ ] 7-11
- [ ] 11-15

- [ ] Other (please state) _____

Name _____

Address _____

Post Code _____

Post

We select a winner in our give-away four times a year and all entries will be automatically entered into the next available draw.

David & Charles

David & Charles Ltd, Brunel House, Newton Abbot, Devon TQ12 4PU Registered No. 840995 England.
www.davidandcharles.co.uk

David & Charles Children's Books   GODSFIELD PRESS

Win a FREE book!

RC002

moroccan-style shutters

Focus on Technique

The shutters were made for windows which are not overlooked and therefore do not need to be solid. Situated in an otherwise featureless space, the shutters give focus and interest to the room. The square-patterned fretwork is echoed in the design of the cut-out MDF frame. The frame of the shutter was patinated and textured with real copper powder, known as copper metal filler, although the copper base could also be achieved using a patinating kit (see Materials). The verdigris patination has been achieved by applying the fluid with a brush, then misting with a spray. The patination must be protected against discoloration over time and has been given a clear wax finish, which also produces an extra sheen.

Materials and Equipment

MDF shutter frames
fine wet-and-dry sandpaper
acrylic primer
paintbrushes
matt emulsion paint in pale green
acrylic size
copper powder
teaspoon
jam jar
patinating fluid
matt acrylic varnish
clear beeswax
soft lint-free cloths
fretwork hardboard panel (available
    from timber merchants)
jigsaw with hardboard blade attachment
red oxide primer
metallic paint in copper
hammer
small brass tacks
metal hinges

Preparation

Lightly sand the frames and fill any holes with acrylic primer. When dry, lightly sand again. Paint with pale green emulsion, including all edges, and leave to dry.

1

Apply a generous amount of acrylic size, ensuring it is brushed into every corner. This will stay tacky for some time, so work slowly and carefully.

2

While the size is still tacky, sprinkle the copper powder on a small area with a teaspoon, then brush it into the size. Brush off any excess and save in a separate, clean, dry jar, as it may have become contaminated with dust. Re-size and add powder to any areas you may have missed.

3

Experiment with the copper and patinating fluid on sample boards to assess how to colour your shutters. For the first coat apply the fluid lightly with a brush or spray, working in a well-ventilated area. Follow the manufacturer's guidelines for the time required for the patina to develop.

4

Apply a matt acrylic varnish and, when this is completely dry, apply clear beeswax with a soft cloth, then buff to a soft sheen.

5

You will need to trim the fretwork panel to fit the shape of the shutter frame. This is best done with a hardboard blade attachment and jigsaw. Prepare both sides of the panel by applying a coat of red oxide primer followed by a coat of copper paint, leaving to dry between coats.

6

The fretwork has been left copper-coloured, although you could apply patinating fluid to the copper, then seal and wax it as before. Attach the fretwork panel with brass tacks to the back of the frame and attach to the window frame with hinges.

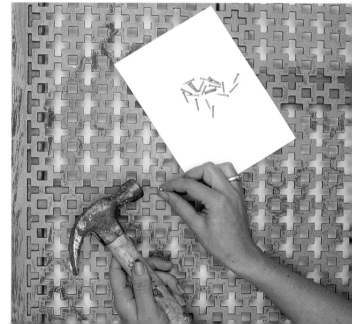

steel-effect column

This plaster column was in a rather sorry state when it was found, with an unresolved, slightly frilly design of questionable character and style. Its glaring whiteness was too blatant, and it looked flat and insubstantial. Given its dramatic new look, it can take its place as an interesting display stand without suggesting any particular period style. It has become a useful plinth to show off beautiful objects, plants or arrangements of flowers. The steel effect used for the main body of the column is very subtle, but as the piece was already rather theatrical it seemed appropriate to try a restrained patina which would not stand out too sharply when seen from a distance, and close up would appear as a simple lustre effect, reflecting light softly and leading the eye upwards to the display.

The ornate foliated capital was painted in a lighter silver shade, and the depth of the relief was emphasized with touches of darker paint to deepen the shadows in the recesses and translucent pale blue lustre to give a lift to the most prominent details.

Given a weighty new character with a subdued metallic paint finish, this light-weight plaster column is now a unique and useful accessory.

steel-effect column

Focus on Technique

Gilding the capital on this column would have been a complicated procedure involving a large amount of silver leaf, so a paint effect was used instead, which is both easier to do and less expensive.

Materials and Equipment

plaster column
all-purpose filler
fine wet-and-dry sandpaper
matt emulsion paint in pale lilac
paintbrushes
oil-based primer in white or pale grey
white spirit
paint kettles
oil-based paint in dark silver
artist's acrylic paints: bright silver, black and
   blue lustre
cellulose decorator's sponge
black shoe polish
soft lint-free cloth

Preparation

Fill any holes or cracks in the plaster and sand the surface smooth.

1 Paint the column completely with pale lilac matt emulsion. Leave to dry, then touch up where necessary to achieve an even covering.

4 Next day, when the oil-based paint is completely dry, sand the surface of the dark silver areas to provide a key for the next application of paint.

5 Brush black acrylic paint over the dark silver. Use a damp sponge to rub this back gently, leaving a random textured finish with the sheen of the silver showing through. Add some touches of blue lustre: this is more transparent and will glaze the surface.

2 Dilute oil-based primer with white spirit and wash this over the areas to receive the oil-based silver paint – the top and body of the column – to help seal the surface. Leave to dry, then paint the column dark silver. After the first coat you may wish to dilute the paint slightly to give it another, smoother layer.

3 While the oil-based paint is drying you can begin to prepare the capital. Because of the intricate detail this may require two coats to cover completely. Stipple bright silver acrylic paint into all the crevices. Leave to dry overnight.

6 Add touches of both colours to the capital, stippling the black paint into the recesses and adding the blue lustre to the areas of high relief to create more texture and patination.

7 Lightly sand areas of the darker silver, then patch with bright silver acrylic paint, dry-brushed in places. Use black shoe polish to give a subtle dark sheen to the body of the column. Wipe on, then buff up with a soft cloth.

woven wire screen

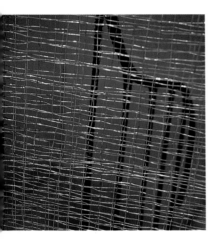

This screen suggests the appearance of steel mesh but is far more interesting. Hand-weaving has given it a quirky, varied texture, with a history and character of its own. It was made using copper wire, some with metal alloy coating, so that it could be patinated, and for the same reason the frame was covered in iron filings. The chemicals used to patinate the copper and iron have been left to dry on the metal, so that the random process of ageing will continue. To give extra colour variations, some zinc and nickel-plated wire was also used. It would be possible to construct the whole screen using galvanized wire, which is cheaper and more easily available, but you would not be able to patinate this in the same way.

This is not a project I would recommend to those who wish instant results, as the work is slow and painstaking. If you like the effect, it would be possible to make a smaller version to hang in a window to catch the light. If the frame is not strong enough the tightening of the wire may cause it to bow, so ensure the battens are thick enough to support the wire, or consider using a metal frame. I love the way the light passes through the weave and hits the different colours. The patinated areas of the mesh are less shiny than the untreated copper, yet still glimmer with a hint of reflected light.

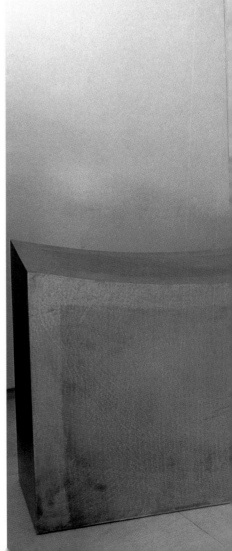

When the screen is used as a room divider, light passes through and hits the woven wire in unusual patterns, demonstrating the intrinsic movement and rhythm in the weave.

Focus on Technique

This project is not for the impatient, as the weaving of the wires is very labour-intensive, but the irregularities of the result give the design a unique character and energy. The patinating fluids have been left on the metal so that the chemical reaction will continue over time.

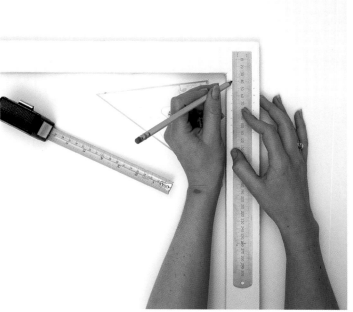

1 Mark the positions of the notches for the wires, 1cm/½in apart all round the frame. Use a hacksaw to cut the notches on the face and the outer edge of the frame.

Materials and Equipment

softwood battens for frame
saw
wood glue
hammer and nails
wet-and-dry sandpaper
acrylic primer
paintbrushes
tape measure
pencil
steel rule
small hacksaw
plastic sheeting
acrylic size
iron filings
spoon
copper wire, some with zinc and nickel coating
wire cutters
pliers
soldering iron and solder (optional)
patinating fluids for iron and copper

Preparation

Make a wooden frame for the screen, using timber that is sufficiently thick to withstand the strain of the tightened wires. Sand and prime the wood and leave to dry. A metal frame could also be used.

4 When all the wires are attached in one direction, add the lengths running across them. These will need to be woven in and out of the other strands, using pliers to thread the wire through.

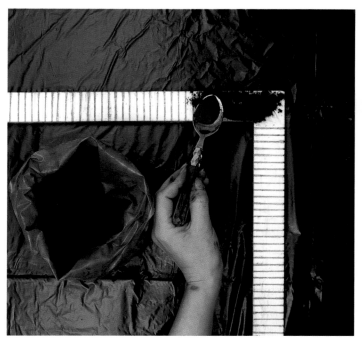

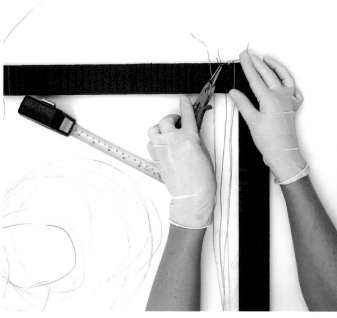

2 Place the frame on plastic sheeting and paint it on all sides with acrylic size. When the size is tacky, sprinkle with iron filings. Shake off any excess and check for any areas that need retouching. Apply more size where necessary and sprinkle on the filings again.

3 Cut a piece of wire double the length of the frame, plus enough to bend around the frame and for twisting the ends. Wind the wire around the frame, bring the ends together at one edge and twist together. Repeat, alternating the colours of the wire.

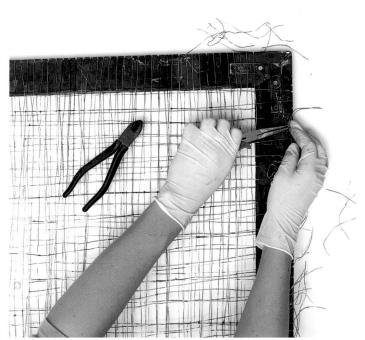

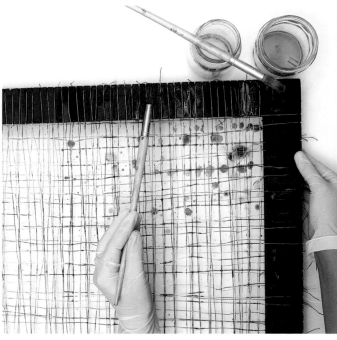

5 When all the wires are in place, undo the ends and pull the strands tight, then twist and trim the ends close to the frame. Solder the ends if you wish to secure them further.

6 Paint the frame and wires with patinating fluids, applying them in alternate bands to create a more interesting effect. Leave the fluids to dry overnight.

'fossil' drawer unit

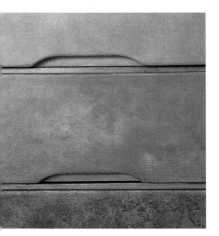

This plain chest of drawers was decorated using a process similar to the traditional technique for imitating tortoiseshell. The effect is achieved by laying down a gold-leaf base which is then washed over with translucent and opaque layers of burnt sienna, yellow ochre and burnt umber paint. Tortoiseshell has a very distinctive pattern which I did not feel was appropriate in this case but, as the technique is such a pleasure to use, I adapted it to give a slightly mottled patination suggesting something halfway between wood grain and a fossilized effect. For extra visual appeal, different colours predominate on alternate drawers.

The oil colours give a soft translucency when applied over a silver base, adding a gentle glistening sheen to the unit. The build-up of layers will give the surface depth and durability which should survive regular handling, and the strength of this finish makes it highly suitable for furniture placed in a kitchen or bathroom. However, as with all painted surfaces, each coat will need time to dry properly. Don't be tempted to cut corners with drying times, as the paints will be reactivated and smear, destroying the unusual depth of texture and colour that you have built up.

An organic-looking paint effect, using a range of natural earth colours with an underlying gleam of silver, lends distinction to this plain piece of furniture.

'fossil' drawer unit

Focus on Technique

The hard finish of the silver base coat needs to be degreased and keyed gently with wire wool to be receptive to the glaze layers. This process will show up any areas of uneven brush strokes, so work carefully and if the base is too rough, add a third dilute coat of silver and leave to dry. The long drying time of the oil paints can be used to your advantage as it will give you time to experiment with effects.

Materials and Equipment

wooden drawer unit

fine wet-and-dry sandpaper

ESP solution (liquid sander)

paintbrushes

paint kettles

white oil-based primer with blue stainer

oil-based paint in silver

white spirit

wire wool

artist's oil paints: burnt sienna, burnt umber and yellow ochre

soft lint-free cloths

black shoe polish

clear beeswax

Preparation

Sand off loose paint then prepare the surface with ESP solution, if necessary, to create a key for the new paint. (This unit had a spray cellulose finish which is difficult to work over without this preparation.)

1

Paint the unit and drawers with pale blue primer, sand lightly and retouch where necessary. Paint the surface with oil-based silver paint. Leave to dry, then apply a second coat of the same paint slightly diluted with white spirit. This will smooth the surface for the next layer.

4

When the paint is almost dry, spatter the surface with white spirit. Leave this to dry for an hour then dab off the spirit and you will find it has removed the paint slightly, creating a 'fossilized' effect.

2

When completely dry, rub down the paint with wire wool, to provide a key for the next layer. If the surface becomes too textured, re-coat with the metal paint to keep the surface smooth, then rub down lightly when dry.

5

Repeat the process until you are satisfied with the effect, then allow to dry. Rub down lightly with wire wool.

3

Dip a brush in white spirit then pick up a touch of oil colour and gently brush the colour on the surface in a circular motion. The different colours should be worked in with some variation of texture and shading. As you add the colours, soften the effect with a cloth to eliminate the brush strokes.

6

Polish the painted surface with black shoe polish to deepen the colour, then apply some clear beeswax for protection and buff to a soft sheen.

gold and silver dresser

Trying to give a contemporary twist to a fairly characterless piece of wooden kitchen furniture seemed an interesting challenge, but as I had no intention of making any structural changes I found I could not ignore the dresser's previous personality and associations. Many kitchen units like this were made of real metal, such as steel, aluminium or zinc, so I decided to parody their utilitarian style by suggesting a functional metal surface yet adding little decorative details and patterns to add some colour and an element of the unexpected.

Using layers of glued paper and foil to achieve this transformation helped to strengthen the weakened joints of the unit, as it had suffered some warping and splitting and might otherwise have become too rickety to use. The paper has also formed a waterproof skin to keep out any more damaging moisture. It is a simple matter to paint sheets of plain white paper in a single metallic colour, and this allows you to create your own colour range. Complex patinas are more difficult to achieve, and the effort hardly seems worth-while when wonderful hand-decorated metallic papers are available from specialist paper suppliers. Use a few sheets of these to enliven the whole piece with additional elements of decoration.

The dresser has been given a flamboyant covering of foil and metallic paper to recreate the retro look of old metal kitchen furniture.

Focus on Technique

The paper chosen to cover most of the unit is a strong
Japanese plant paper with long fibres and good
absorbency. This stretches around the wood and
tightens as it dries to hold together slightly uneven
panels and weakened joints. It is strengthened and
waterproofed with a liberal coat of PVA glue. Painted
layout paper can be used decoratively over the
stronger Japanese paper. The aluminium foil used is
thicker than domestic kitchen foil and must be
ordered through specialist suppliers. It should be
limited to areas of occasional use as it can scratch or
tear: if it becomes marked, polish with a soft cloth
and methylated spirit.

Materials and Equipment

wooden kitchen unit
wet-and-dry sandpaper
all-purpose filler
methylated spirit
acrylic primer
paintbrushes
tape measure
Japanese handmade paper
layout paper
water-based paints and powders: gold and silver
cellulose decorator's sponge (optional)
spray paints: gold and silver (optional)
pencil
steel rule
masking tape
PVA glue
fine-gauge craft aluminium foil
scissors
contact adhesive
soft lint-free cloth or wooden spoon
handmade metallic papers
satin acrylic varnish

Preparation

The dresser should be sanded and filled, stripping
back the old surface as much as possible. In this case,
one of the doors was discarded as it was in bad
condition. The hinges were removed and the shelves
left open. The zinc top of the dresser was wiped
down with methylated spirit. Paint the wood with
two coats of acrylic primer. Measure the areas to be
covered with paper to check that the pieces you have
chosen are large enough.

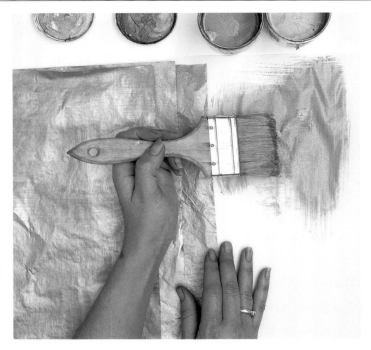

1 Lay out the Japanese handmade papers and layout
paper on a flat surface and paint with a selection of
gold and silver colours. You can dilute the paints,
applying with a brush or sponge, or use spray paint.
Leave to dry.

4 Aluminium foil was used to cover the edges of the
frame and shelves. Mark the required size with pencil
and then cut out. Apply contact adhesive to the
primed wood and to the back of the foil, stick the
foil down and smooth with a cloth or the back of a
wooden spoon to ensure a good contact.

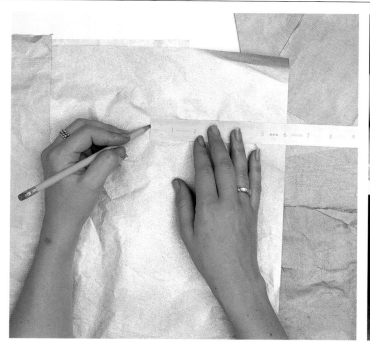

2 When you have decided where you wish to use the different colours, cut or tear the papers into the appropriate sizes. This dresser has predominantly silver papers on the exterior and gold for the interior.

3 Try out your ideas by attaching the papers with tape. When you are happy with the balance, stick them down using PVA glue diluted 1:2 with water. Apply the glue both to the primed surface and to the back of the paper. When the base papers are dry add decoration with alternate colours and papers.

5 Use handmade metallic papers to add decorative details, cutting them into strips then into small squares and circles.

6 Apply the decorations using PVA glue diluted 1:1 with water. Leave the glue to dry then brush on several coats of satin acrylic varnish all over the paper covering. Leave to dry between coats. The foil does not need any protection, but can be cleaned of varnish and glue with methylated spirit.

bronze-patina box

This is a wonderful effect, and one that is possible to make look amazingly realistic. Bronze can be found in an astonishing range of colours and textured finishes. Cast metal sculpture and artefacts are patinated using heat and chemicals as well as natural ageing processes, and go through a whole spectrum of colour variations. This version has been chosen to allow the box to fit easily into any colour scheme and to give it weight and substance. The textured bronze powdered paints give the surface a degree of illusory depth and feel almost authentic when you pass your hand over the surface, except that the box feels warm while bronze itself can be extremely cold and unyielding.

There is no single prescriptive method that will guarantee a successful result: use trial and error until you are happy with the effect. The more you work over the surface the more interesting it will look, so you do not have to worry about going too far if you find you are building up the layers repeatedly. As with all paint effects, the paint needs to be layered thinly to prevent any cracking or peeling: each coat must have enough drying time to harden off properly to give a really durable surface.

Plain MDF boxes offer a smooth surface for painting, and make useful side tables or seats. The shapes are unassuming, with nothing to detract from the beauty of the finish. Place with real metal surfaces for an interesting combination of textures.

bronze-patina box

Focus on Technique

The patinating process can be achieved without the use of any chemicals as bronze powders come in a huge range of colours. Mixed with a variety of binders, these can create wonderful and unusual combinations of effects. Patinating fluid has been used here, however, because it helps to generate more varied textures and the oxidizing process gives a soft powdery feel to the surface. If you want a more random finish you can leave the fluid on overnight, but I wished to control the process so only allowed it to remain active for about an hour.

Materials and Equipment

MDF box
all-purpose filler
wet-and-dry sandpaper
acrylic primer
paintbrushes
board for samples
iron filings
copper powder (copper metal filler)
water-based paint in matt black
paint kettles and shallow containers
bronze powders in a selection of colours: copper,
    brown, orange gold, green and fire copper
selection of binders: PVA glue, sanding sealer
    or shellac
cellulose decorator's sponges
patinating fluids: iron and bronze
wire wool
artist's acrylic paint in deep bronze
acrylic interference medium or transparent
    lustre paint: orange and green
soft lint-free cloths
black shoe polish (optional)
clear beeswax

Preparation

Fill, sand and prime the box with acrylic primer. Re-coat and sand until the surface is completely smooth and blemish-free. Prepare a sample board to try out textures and colour variations.

1 Sprinkle some iron filings and copper powder into the black paint and stir in well to disperse. Cover the box in the mix using a combination of brushing and stippling. Leave to dry then retouch where necessary to achieve sufficient coverage.

4 Tone down the patina with a coat of bronze acrylic paint diluted with water and applied with a sponge.

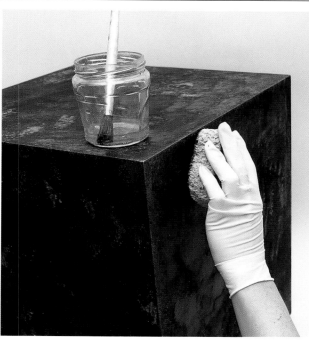

2 Referring to your sample board, mix some of the bronze powders with binders and a small amount of water. Apply these to the box by stippling and texturing with brushes and sponges in a series of broken cloud shapes. Allow to dry, then continue to add colours to create a richly textured surface.

3 Using a sponge, dab the iron and bronze patinating fluids lightly over the surface. After a while you will begin to see the oxidation beginning; when you want to control the effect, wash off the fluid with water and another sponge. Remove excessive oxidation by rubbing with wire wool.

5 Still using a sponge, dab over areas of the surface with the acrylic interference medium or transparent lustre paint in orange.

6 Dilute the green interference/lustre paint with water then wash over the whole surface, to help seal the effect and give a subtle green sheen. Wax the surface with black shoe polish and clear beeswax.

details

introduction

Metallic effects can be enjoyed purely for their decoration, as in this patinated wire-mesh cushion.

The projects in this chapter deal with a selection of objects that might be introduced as adornments to a decorative scheme once it has been put together, creating visual highlights and a focus of interest. Such details need to echo the chosen colours and theme of a room while adding a special touch of unique individual vision. Some may be functional as well as decorative while others – while not remotely useful – can be a way to express your own creative interests, style and ideas, to demonstrate your sense of humour or conjure up happy memories.

This area of decoration is perhaps the one in which gilding and other metallic effects are likely to be found in most homes: in picture frames, boxes, candlesticks and other ornamental finishing touches. However, my intention here has been to work not with precious ornaments but with the most ordinary things. Each decorative idea involves a form of recycling and the transformation of an everyday object or material into something beautiful and unusual. This is the group of projects I see as a true expression of the extraordinary transitions that can take place when an ordinary object becomes a prized possession, just because of the addition of the glitter of gold or silver. A group of slightly dull but nicely shaped dried leaves have been given the Midas touch and have become the decorative focus of a room; an

Flexible craft mesh was embellished with small pieces of coloured aluminium to make a lampshade.

old roof tile has been turned into an unusual sconce and is now vibrant and sparkling, with candlelight reflected from every facet of its craggy surface; an old lamp has been stripped down and revamped with a dramatic and colourful mesh shade. Such unpromising raw materials represent the sort of objects that accumulate in every household: though they do not merit display as they are, you may enjoy them for their unusual shapes or interesting textures. If you look at them with a fresh eye you may find that they can be turned into glittering treasures that light up a space with the addition of a few leaves of gold, or even the shimmer of more workaday metals such as aluminium and brass.

Metal leaf is applied to glass, which can then be marked with patterns, in a technique known as verre églomisé.

These projects use a variety of techniques, from the special skill of gilding on glass to create an ethereal work of art, to stitching and moulding metal mesh and incising and decorating gesso. They demonstrate the adaptability of metallic finishes to surfaces of all kinds, as well as showing how such effects can bring disparate objects together to form decorative groups.

Your immediate home environment is a space in which you should be able to choose colours, objects and textures that make you feel relaxed, happy and stimulated. Whether you introduce them on a large or a small scale, metallic finishes add flashes of glamour and touches of elegant detail. The materials used to add this sheen and brilliance are exciting to work with and can result in some spectacular transformations.

Textural interest is created by laying different shades of gold and silver leaf over a carved gesso background.

silver candle sconce

The curve and tapered shape of an old roof-tile suggested a new use for it as a reflector for a candle sconce. The worn terracotta surface of the tile was perfect for gilding when the loose dust had been removed. In its natural state it would absorb much of the light, but now the candlelight dances across the textured dimpled surface and is reflected outwards; shadows remain in the indentations and the light reveals areas of smoother glittering aluminium leaf.

The finish would be able to withstand mild weather conditions and a certain amount of damp, so it would be suitable for use outside on a sheltered wall. A hole can be drilled through the tile to hang it on a wall or post.

The curlicue fitting for the candle was taken from a ready-made wrought iron sconce, and was painted with silver spray paint to match the tile, then patinated with spirit dyes.

Rustic terracotta and wrought iron, transformed with aluminium leaf, fit effortlessly into a modern urban garden setting.

silver candle sconce

Focus on Technique

The dull worn surface of a terracotta tile has been revitalized with the addition of aluminium leaf, then mellowed with the transparent colouring of dark spirit dyes and shellac. It could be prepared with home-made gesso and bole to take water-gilding if you wish, as the metal leaf would look wonderful burnished before patination. Aluminium leaf does not tarnish so there is no need to varnish it but you could protect against scratches with wax polish.

Materials and Equipment

wrought-iron candle sconce
wire wool
black iron primer
paintbrushes
old roof tile
soft brush
clear shellac
acrylic gesso
paint kettle
fine wet-and-dry sandpaper
artist's acrylic paint in blue
acrylic size
aluminium leaf
gilder's tip (optional)
pounce bag with whiting (optional)
gilder's knife and cushion, or scissors
silver spray paint
spirit dyes: black, blue, brown and purple
soft lint-free cloths
methylated spirit

Preparation

Dismantle the wrought-iron fitment, rub down and prime with black iron primer.

1 Rub over the tile with wire wool to remove any loose dust and smooth the surface. Brush off with a soft brush. Seal with a coat of clear shellac so that the surface is not too porous and the finish will be protected from any moisture seepage.

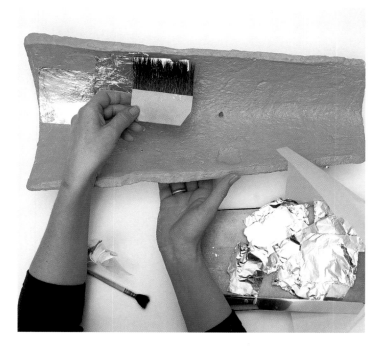

4 When the size is tacky, begin to add the aluminium leaf. Use a gilder's tip or cover your fingers in whiting and lift the loose leaf on to the size. The leaf can be cut with a gilder's knife or with scissors: with smaller pieces it will be easier to get the leaf to follow the curve of the tile.

2 When the shellac is dry, apply two solid coats of acrylic gesso. Alternate the direction of the brush strokes and lightly sand between coats once dry.

3 Apply another layer of gesso mixed with blue acrylic paint. When dry, sand lightly and paint the tile with acrylic size.

5 Spray the iron fitment silver and leave to dry. Paint a mixture of spirit dyes on to the tile, then gently rub and wipe the surface with a soft cloth dipped in a little methylated spirit. This will lift the darker colour off the raised areas, leaving it in the recesses.

gilded objects

One of the wonders of gilding is just how easy it is to transform the humblest of forms into glistening, glamorous, shimmeringly precious pieces with an improved innate value. The gilded objects here create a bright focal point in the room, and will bring opulence to any interior. The pieces reflect light, and will sparkle and catch the eye as you move about the room. This new appearance of glamour will make you re-assess the original objects and appreciate their simple, sculptural forms in a new way.

Any object can be given this treatment. Here, a selection of natural organic objects was used – pebbles, gourds, sticks, leaves and wooden pots. Their varying shapes and sizes work together to create a glistening still life. Experiment with different objects – spheres, cubes and other geometric forms, for example – and with real and imitation metal leaf. The different qualities of leaf are obvious to the eye when displayed together.

Flickering firelight sets off this collection of gilded objects to perfection. Flames are reflected in the glowing surfaces, emphasizing their metallic qualities. Metal leaf has transformed humble objects – sticks, leaves, gourds, wooden bowls – into priceless sculpture.

gilded objects

Focus on Technique

This traditional gilding technique demonstrates the magic of the Midas touch, turning the plainest of objects into something precious and beautiful. The technique of applying thin metal leaf is easy to master, and proves how simple it is to transform base materials into gold! Make sure you work in a dust-free environment.

Materials and Equipment

selection of objects to be gilded, such as gourds, bowls, vases etc.

wet-and-dry sandpaper

paintbrushes

clear shellac

gesso, either pre-made acrylic or home-made gesso (see Techniques)

hog's hair brush

bole in red, yellow and blue (see Techniques)

12-hour size or acrylic size

selection of transfer leaf: gold, silver, white gold and Dutch metal

scissors

gilder's mop

1 To prepare the objects for gilding, sand off any loose or flaky surfaces, then seal the areas to be gilded with clear shellac. Leave to dry, then lightly sand the surface again.

4 Cut up the transfer leaf into manageable pieces with a pair of sharp scissors. Lay the first piece on the sized surface and lightly rub the back to release the leaf. Repeat with the remaining pieces. Each piece should slightly overlap the last to ensure there are no gaps.

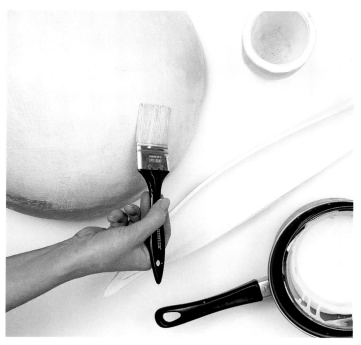

2 Build up at least four layers of gesso by applying with a hog's hair brush. If using acrylic gesso, leave to dry and lightly sand between each coat. If using home-made gesso, each subsequent layer can be applied while the previous one is drying. Sand using wet-and-dry sandpaper with a film of water.

3 Paint the surfaces with bole, using different colours for different objects. Use blue bole for an object to be covered in silver leaf and yellow or red for gold leaf. Leave to dry, then apply 12-hour or acrylic size to the surface. If using 12-hour size, this will need to be applied the night before you intend to gild.

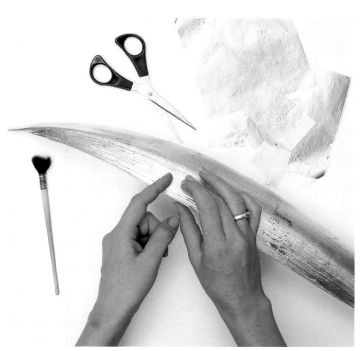

5 Use a different metal leaf for each object and experiment with different base colours to see the effects you can achieve. When the surface is covered, repair any gaps by re-sizing and adding small patches of leaf. Any size left over the leaf will discolour the metal, so make sure it is covered completely.

6 Objects covered in Dutch metal will need to be protected from tarnishing. To do so, apply thin coats of clear shellac.

mesh lampshade

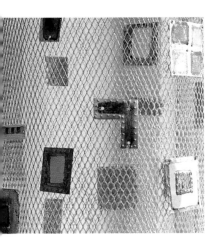

Traditional punched tin work was often used to make lanterns, with a decorative design of tiny holes pierced through a metal cylinder which protected the candle flame from the wind while letting through small pinpoints of light. From this folk-art technique came the germ of the idea for a thoroughly modern lampshade.

Its decoration consists of fragments of thin aluminium sheet, cut into a variety of simple shapes and then punched and stitched to a striking, tall cylinder of flexible mesh.

Every part of this lamp gently glimmers and sparkles. The delicate metallic mesh has been strengthened and given substance with mica lustre flakes, thickly sprinkled over a coat of shellac. The decorated mini-plaques, which are gently curved to fit the cylindrical shape, gleam with multi-coloured patterns painted in translucent spirit dyes. Use a soft-effect bulb to show off this original lampshade best – against a pale wall it looks magical. This easy idea could inspire a multitude of other designs using wire mesh and aluminium: it would suit lamps of any shape and size, and the same principles could be applied to make containers and baskets.

Small aluminium plaques stitched all over the mesh shade cast delicate scattered shadows across a white wall.

mesh lampshade

Focus on Technique
The spirit dyes used here to colour the aluminium will not be very durable if they are likely to be handled often, but they give a unique translucent finish, allowing the aluminium to show through as a subtle sheen. For stronger colours use enamels, which will give solid colours, or glass paints, which will be more transparent than enamels but more permanent than spirit dyes. The application of shellac, bronze powders and Dutch metal leaf offers more scope for a variety of effects.

Materials and Equipment
old cylindrical lampshade
flexible craft wire mesh
tape measure
pencil
scissors
needle and invisible thread
clear shellac
paintbrushes
mica flakes
spoon
0.3mm aluminium sheet
steel rule
craft knife
cutting mat
bradawl
methylated spirit
soft lint-free cloths
selection of spirit dyes
bronze powders
transfer Dutch metal leaf in gold

Preparation
Strip off the fabric or parchment from an old cylindrical lampshade and clean and recycle the top and bottom rings to shape your shade.

1

Measure and mark the amount of wire mesh you will need to fit the lampshade rings, allowing an overlap for the side seam. Try not to stretch the mesh, which is flexible and could be easily moulded to the wrong shape. Trim the mesh with scissors.

2

Hold the lampshade ring inside the mesh cylinder and bend the edge around the ring to hold it securely in place, then stitch with invisible thread. Repeat with the other ring. Use invisible thread to stitch the seam down the length of the shade.

3

Brush the mesh with clear shellac. Before the shellac dries, sprinkle it with mica flakes. Repeat until you have covered the whole shade with a textured layer of flakes.

4

Cut two 2.5cm/1in wide strips from the aluminium sheet to make the trimming for the top and bottom of the shade, then draw decorative shapes on another piece of aluminium and cut out with scissors or a craft knife. Punch the backs of the shapes with details using a bradawl. Use the bradawl to make fixing holes at each corner and along the length of the strips.

5

Degrease the pieces of aluminium with methylated spirit and decorate with a variety of colours and effects. Bronze powders can be mixed with shellac and diluted with methylated spirit. Add Dutch metal leaf by painting on shellac (instead of size) then press the leaf on as the shellac becomes tacky.

6

Curve the decorations slightly and use invisible thread to stitch them at random to the mesh. Stitch the strips to the top and bottom of the shade.

brass mesh cushion

The mesh is an illusory material which appears light but is actually quite heavy. It is very flexible and malleable and can be moulded and bent quite easily. Because it is woven like fabric, I could not resist the idea of moulding it into a plump and very striking cushion: it would certainly provide back support but would not be very comfortable.

It will hold its shape without any filling but, continuing the analogy with upholstery, I have filled it with metal curls – though these are not springs but scraps of metal waste from a lathe. A good alternative filling would be some light, translucent fabric, paper or foil, which can be seen easily when light passes through the mesh. The trimming is a length of antique fringing that includes some real silver thread to make it suitably weighty for this unusual cushion.

Brass patinating fluid was painted on to the brass to create a bold design with a heraldic look. By carefully controlling the amount of chemical used you can vary the extent of the patination, retaining some of the sheen of the brass.

Woven brass with a texture reminiscent of
coarse linen has been turned into a witty
visual pun.

brass mesh cushion

Focus on Technique

The mesh is soft enough to be cut with scissors, but it will blunt the blades so use an old pair. You can use patinating fluid to shade the colour of the brass in a subtle way as the mesh is very dense. As the chemicals are left to dry on the mesh the metal will continue to age.

Materials and Equipment

brass mesh

tape measure

pencil

old scissors

steel rule

fine wire

pliers

brass patinating fluid

old paintbrush

cushion filling (see Preparation)

antique silver thread fringing

large needle

invisible thread

Preparation

Contact a local tool-making company if you want to fill the cushion with curls of metal waste, or collect some other suitable materials, such as ribbons of transparent fabric, strips of metal foil, pieces of wire or paper.

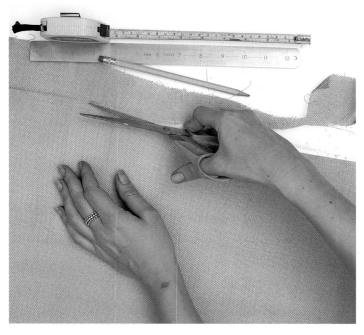

1 Decide on the size of the cushion and mark out a rectangle, double the length, to be folded in half. Allow extra for the turnings around the sides, and bear in mind that the cushion shape will reduce the finished size. Cut out with scissors.

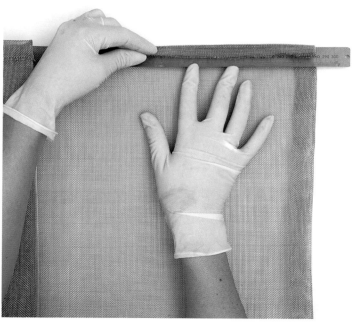

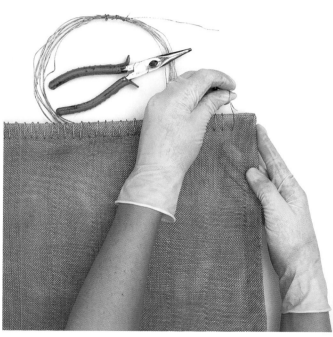

2 Fold the mesh in half and use your hands to push the sides out into a cushion shape. Fold in the raw edges, bending the mesh over a steel rule.

3 Use fine wire to oversew the edges with regularly spaced stitches, weaving the wire by hand through the mesh. If you want to fill the cushion, leave part of one side open.

4 Mark a simple design for the patination with a pencil and a steel rule. Use an old brush to wash the patinating fluid over the mesh, concentrating on the outer edges of each area so that the colour shades into a lighter centre. Repeat as necessary, rinsing the brush between layers.

5 Leave the fluid to dry, then fill the cushion and stitch the opening. Attach the fringe trimming using invisible thread.

incised gesso plaque

This abstract three-dimensional piece was created using techniques intended to give texture to large flat areas of gilding by incising the underlying gesso with carving tools. The method can provide balance and pattern in burnished areas, and is a traditional way of adding detail to gilded picture frames. If the gilding is to be patinated, the incised areas will hold more colour, and contribute to a more interesting surface for light to play over. Punch work is another way of cutting into gesso, traditionally used in icons to pick out haloes and other details.

If the gesso is built up to at least 5mm/¼in, very beautiful low relief carving is possible, but it is a painstaking process. Another method, known as *pastiglio*, refers to the painting or drawing on of shapes and patterns: a brush is loaded with liquid gesso which is flowed on to a flat gesso surface, giving a smooth, rounded effect.

The irregular circular shape of this piece suggested the use of organic, abstract decoration, rather than anything too rigid or graphic. The patterns were copied from references relating to pebbles and shells, with fluid shapes and textures contained within an organized design. The gilding is in silver and gold leaf in various shades. The three-dimensional effect has been exaggerated by mounting the smaller circle on a block so that it 'floats' over the base. The plaque was then patinated with bleach and spirit dyes.

Abstract patterns carved into a gesso surface create a rich texture for gilding and allow light to play across the different planes and textures of the piece.

incised gesso plaque

Focus on Technique

Unless you are very experienced in working with home-made gesso, I suggest using an acrylic gesso base for this piece, although you will find the surface is more difficult to cut into, and may chip off if you attempt any fine work. Home-made gesso takes longer to prepare and apply but gives a fantastic soft surface for cutting. It is possible to use clay modelling or linoleum cutting tools for incising gesso, but do try the technique on a sample board first, as you may be disappointed with the uneven finish until you find your rhythm.

If you use oil size for gilding you must be careful when patinating as methylated spirit may cause the size to lift, and bleach may cause it to re-activate. If you intend to use both methods of patination it may be best to use acrylic size.

Materials and Equipment

sample board

sketch of design

two circular wooden panels

wet-and-dry sandpaper

wire wool

methylated spirit

acrylic primer

paintbrushes

acrylic gesso

pencil

cutting tools

cellulose decorator's sponges

blue stainer

paint kettle

acrylic size

transfer and loose silver leaf

transfer Dutch metal leaf: silver and gold

pounce bag with whiting (optional)

bleach

soft lint-free cloths

spirit dyes: black, blue and brown

clear shellac

Preparation

Prepare a sample board with acrylic gesso and experiment with cutting tools and ideas. Sketch a design for the wall piece: this could flow from one circular panel to the other, or the two could be contrasted.

1 Sand the wooden panels. Degrease by rubbing with wire wool dipped in methylated spirit.

4 Place the small circle on top of the large one and draw out your design in pencil on both panels.

2 Prime with two coats of acrylic primer, sanding lightly between coats.

3 Paint the panels with successive thin coats of acrylic gesso, leaving to dry at each stage and sanding between coats. Build up the surface to a depth of about 5mm/¼in.

5 Cut out the details of the design using sharp gouges and flat chisels. Try to cut deeply but do not remove all the layers of gesso, as this may leave the raised areas loose and cause them to flake off.

6 Wash off the pencil marks with a damp sponge then re-coat the surface with acrylic primer tinted with blue stainer. Brush on the paint as smoothly as possible, without adding texture to the surface.

7 When the primer is dry, paint the surface with acrylic size and leave until tacky.

8 Cover the panel in silver leaf. Cut the squares into pieces that are small enough to lay on easily. You may wish to work in sections, using different metals on alternating textured areas. Rub the backing of the transfer leaf to release it before removing the paper.

10 Wash very dilute bleach over the panel, leave a moment, then rinse off with a damp cloth. Work back over some sections with a brush to darken. The water may cause the acrylic size to release, so do not saturate the panel and remove the bleach quickly.

11 Apply a wash of spirit dyes and methylated spirit over the surface, then wipe back with a soft cloth dipped in methylated spirit.

9 Re-size some areas with a small brush and add details of gold leaf for interest. If the leaf is cut small it will be easy to place over particular sections. If you are using loose leaf, cover your fingers in whiting to prevent it sticking.

12 You can also spatter the surface with methylated spirit to give an aged effect. When dry, protect the plaque with at least one layer of clear shellac.

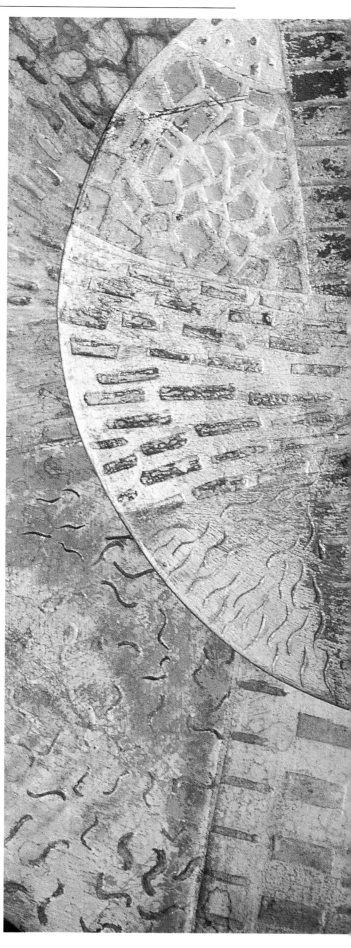

verre églomisé panel

Verre églomisé refers to the technique of gilding patterns onto glass. Silver leaf may be used, as here, for the main area, with the addition of decorative details in gold leaf, or the reverse. A variation of this technique involves drawing a design on to the back of the gilded glass then painting it with carefully applied patinating fluid to age and discolour the gilding in a controlled way. An expert in this process can achieve wonderful toning and shading, but it is a highly skilled technique. The earliest examples can be found on artefacts as far back as Roman times, and these were fired to fuse the decoration between two layers of glass. In the 18th century a new technique was developed in which the reverse of the glass was gilded and decorated, and was then protected by a layer of paint (traditionally black) and this is the method generally used today. Decoration can be added by inscribing the dry gilding so that the paint shows through the inscribed areas. The gilding is seen through the glass, which becomes a kind of mirror, though the reflections are softly gleaming rather than sharp and clear.

The pane of leaded and gilded glass, like a precious ancient mirror, throws back ghostly, disjointed reflections.

verre églomisé panel

Focus on Technique

The glass is gilded using loose silver and gold leaf. The squares of silver leaf can be picked up straight from the book using a gilder's tip. If you have problems doing this, wipe the tip under your chin or across your forehead to add a little grease. If this fails, use a touch of petroleum jelly. The surface will be double-gilded so your first attempt need not be too perfect. Small breaks in the silver will reveal the colour of the paint on the back and add character to the glass.

Materials and Equipment

leaded glass window
methylated spirit
soft lint-free cloths
gelatine capsule
distilled water
heatproof bowl and jug
paintbrushes
gilder's tip
loose leaf: silver and gold
gilder's mop
wooden skewer
carbon paper (optional)
gilder's cushion
gilder's knife
oil-based paint in black (or other colour)

Preparation

Clean the front and back of the glass repeatedly with methylated spirit and soft cloths to remove all traces of dust and grease.

1

To make the size, use half a gelatine capsule and 300ml/½ pint distilled water. Warm a small amount of the water in which to dissolve the capsule, then add the rest cold. Raise one side of the glass so any excess size will run away from the leaf. Paint the size on to the first section of the glass.

2

Use a gilder's tip to pick a piece of silver leaf straight from the book. Place the tip parallel to the glass and lay off in a quick, smooth motion. If the silver breaks or folds remove it with a wet brush. Apply the size to the next section and repeat until the glass is covered. Leave to dry.

3

Hold the glass over steam for a few seconds to allow the size to 'cure': this will help the leaf to settle more firmly, smoothing out wrinkles and making closer contact with the glass. Now repeat the process to double-gild. Apply less size and brush it on quickly to avoid lifting the first coat. Leave to dry again.

4

Use a gilder's mop to dust off any loose leaf, then mark out your design. Inscribe it with a wooden point so you do not scrape the glass. Do this freehand if possible, otherwise use carbon paper – the design will be in reverse. Try not to touch the surface with your hands. Dust off the leaf you have removed.

5

At this stage you can just paint over the silver so that the paint colour shows through the incised design. Alternatively, gild again with loose gold leaf. Repeat the steps as before, but you will need only small pieces of leaf so have some cut squares ready to use.

6

The gilding should now be coated in an even layer of oil-based paint in your choice of colour (black is traditional). Any gaps in the gilding will show the colour. The paint will protect against scratches and tarnishing.

technical information

introduction

The production of metal leaf involves a process of heating, rolling and beating. To make a range of colours, gold leaf is alloyed with other metal such as silver and copper, a process which also makes it harder. Pure gold is very soft, but will not tarnish – one reason it is so highly valued.

Loose leaf is usually reserved for water-gilding, as it can be burnished to a high sheen. Transfer leaf is easier to handle but has less lustre, due to the pressure involved in applying the leaf to the backing paper. For this reason it is normally used in oil-gilding, which is not suitable for burnishing. Dutch metal leaf, a much cheaper alternative, can be used in much the same way but requires sealing with shellac or varnish because it will otherwise tarnish, as will copper leaf.

The correct preparation of the surface to be gilded is of the utmost importance. Water-gilding requires a smooth 'cushion' of gesso (a mix of size and whiting) to enable it to be burnished to a gleaming finish, as an uneven surface would result in the leaf tearing when rubbed with the burnisher. Gilding with oil or acrylic size may also be applied to gesso, but as no burnishing is involved the preparation of an absolutely smooth surface is less critical, and you may prefer to use ready-made materials such as acrylic gesso, acrylic primer and water or oil-based paints.

The use of gesso allows you to texture the surface before gilding, creating low or high relief. Gesso is traditionally coloured with layers of coloured clay, called bole. Red and black bole are used for water-gilding as they are the best for burnishing, while yellow bole is used for oil-gilding. However, in traditional gilding yellow may be used on areas that are difficult to water-gild in case the coverage is not complete: since yellow is closest in colour to gold, any faults are less obvious.

Some of the projects in this book use paint rather than gilding to achieve metallic finishes, and these ideas should be seen as starting points for your own experiments. Metal powders are another alternative. The term 'bronze powders' covers the spectrum of different powders made from bronze, copper, silver, aluminium or metal alloys. Metal powders, wire and mesh can all be patinated using chemicals to accelerate the natural effects of exposure to air and moisture.

Flakes of mica or celluloid are another way of adding sparkle. A range of these can be bought from good artists' suppliers, in powder form or ready-mixed. Lustre colours, or acrylic interference medium, can also be used to help give an iridescent or opalescent finish. They produce beautifully subtle effects.

I strongly recommend experimentation with all gilding and patinating techniques but you first need to master the basics so that you know how to push the boundaries. Specialized skills are always best explored by following a practical course: any problems you encounter can more easily be assessed, discussed and understood when working alongside a good teacher.

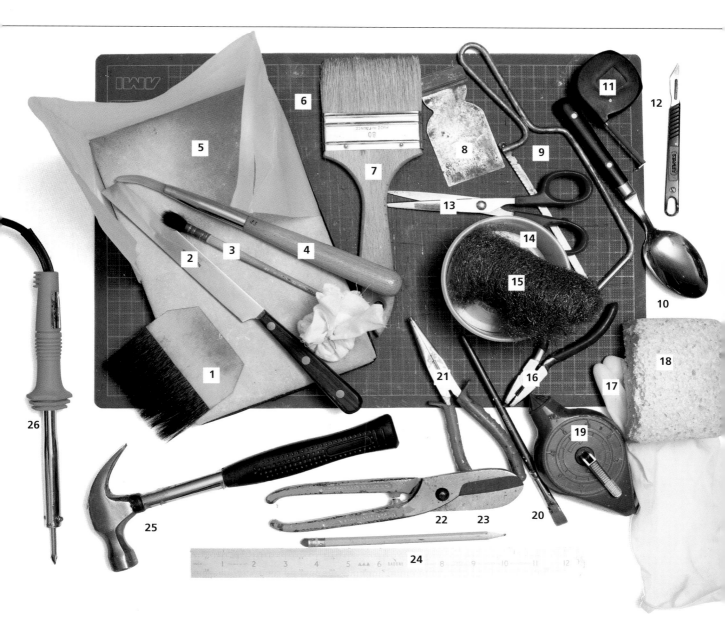

equipment

Much of the equipment used in this book is fairly straightforward and will be familiar to anyone accustomed to doing decorating projects. Specialist equipment, however, is required for traditional gilding techniques, and is included in the list below.

11 gilder's tip
for lifting loose leaf on to the sized surface

12 gilder's knife
for cutting and lifting loose leaf

13 gilder's mop
for dusting off loose-leaf flakes after gilding

14 gilder's agate burnisher
for burnishing and adding shine to water-gilding

15 gilder's cushion
for preparing and cutting loose leaf

16 re-sealing cutting mat

17 hog's hair brush

18 continental filler knife

19 D-saw

10 spoon

11 tape measure

12 scalpel

13 scissors

14 small paint container

15 wire wool

16 pliers or wire cutters

17 protective gloves

18 decorator's cellulose sponge

19 chalk line

20 artist's brush

21 long-nose pliers

22 sheet metal cutters

23 pencil

24 steel rule

25 hammer

26 soldering iron

materials

Surface metallic effects can be created with a wide range of different materials. The ideas in this book use materials ranging from traditional metal leaf to acrylic paints and powders. Metal leaf comes loose or as a transfer, from the costly gold leaf through to less expensive Dutch metal or aluminium. Bronze powders come in a range of colours (not just bronze) and can be mixed with a binder such as PVA glue before application. A wide range of metallic acrylic- and oil-based paints are also available.

1 **green acrylic metallic paint**
2 **oil-based metallic paint**
3 **spirit dyes**
4 **methylated spirit**
5 **12-hour oil size**
6 **acrylic size**
7 **shellac**
8 **bronze acrylic metallic paint**
9 **mica flakes**
10 **Dutch metal leaf in 25-sheet pack**
11 **transfer silver leaf**
12 **Dutch metal loose gold leaf**
13 **transfer copper leaf**
14 **Dutch metal transfer leaf**
15 **loose copper leaf**
16 **glitter**
17 **metallic acrylic paint suitable for patinating fluid**
18 **bronze powder: antique gold**
19 **bronze powders: gold and fire copper**
20 **loose gold leaf in 25-sheet pack**
21 **loose silver leaf**
22 **copper leaf flakes**
23 **loose aluminium leaf**
24 **bronze powder: green**
25 **bronze powder: yellow gold**
26 **metallic powder: copper**
27 **metallic powder: red gold**
28 **copper powder**
29 **iron filings**
30 **acrylic metallic and lustre paint**

materials

The introduction of metallic effects in the home need not be limited to surface applications only. Some of the pieces in this book use reclaimed materials such as aluminium sheeting or wire mesh, which may be treated with patinating fluid to oxidize the metal and create new surface patterns and colours. Some materials have been used to replicate a traditional treatment, with stucco used in place of gesso for example. In other instances, a metallic paper has been used to echo a utilitarian zinc surface. Use the items below as a springboard for your own interpretations.

1 **artist's oil and watercolour paints**

2 **brush-on patinating fluid for copper**

3 **spray-on patinating fluid**

4 **brush-on patinating fluid for iron**

5 **reclaimed aluminium lithography plates**

6 **self-adhesive bookbinders' foil**

7 **thin aluminium foil, from roll**

8 **wire wool**

9 **PVA glue**

10 **metallic-effect paper**

11 **bronze mesh, with copper and brass wire**

12 **craft mesh, with aluminium wire**

13 **invisible thread**

14 **gelatine**

15 **whiting**

16 and 17 **rabbit-skin size granules**

18 **copper, brass and aluminium wire**

19 **contact adhesive**

20 **powder pigment, for stucco**

21 **plaster stucco mix**

traditional gilding techniques

preparing size

To achieve the absolutely smooth surface required for water-gilding, you will need to use home-made gesso, for which you will first need to prepare some size. This is best made from rabbit-skin glue, which is available in powder, granule or sheet form. Once mixed, the size can be left to cool then transferred to a plastic container and stored in the fridge until you need it. Do not store it for too long, however, as it will eventually start to rot and smell appalling.

An alternative size, usually reserved for gilding on glass, can be made from gelatine, supplied in capsules. Traditionally, isinglass (fish glue) was used for this purpose, but it is difficult to obtain. To mix the size, use half a gelatine capsule and 300ml/½ pint distilled water. Warm a small amount of the water in which to dissolve the capsule, then add the rest cold.

Materials and Equipment
rabbit-skin glue, spoon, bowl and saucepan or bain-marie, whiting, sieve, wooden panel, hog's hair brush, strips of fine linen

1 Soak the rabbit-skin glue in a little water to soften it, then add about ten parts water to one part glue and place the mixture in a bowl over a pan of simmering water or a bain-marie to liquefy. The size must be supervised and stirred while it is warming, and any scum should be removed from the surface.

2 Before applying gesso, the area to be gilded should be prepared with size. Warm in a bowl over simmering water, then add about a teaspoon of whiting to 120ml/4fl oz of size. Stir gently and leave briefly to allow any air bubbles to rise.

3 Apply the size with a hog's hair brush, leave to dry, then rub back gently. The mixture can also be used to attach fabric strips to the corners of a panel to reinforce the joints. Soak strips of linen in the size mix and press tightly around the corners of the panel. Leave to dry.

preparing gesso and bole

Gesso is applied in a series of thin layers, and these must all be taken from the same batch so that the consistency of the mixture is constant: the gesso should be made freshly and the surface completed in the same day. As the gesso needs to be kept warm while you are working, you will probably need to add a spoonful of water to the mixture from time to time as the water evaporates, otherwise the resulting surface may become brittle and flake off.

Clay bole is painted over the gesso to add a sealing layer before the size is applied to take the leaf. It provides colour enrichment and makes a pliable cushion to assist the burnishing process. Bole can be bought as a paste suspended in water, and different colours need to be mixed with slightly different amounts of size: one part yellow to about ⅚ part size and one part red to about ¾ part size.

Materials and Equipment
whiting, sieve, bowls, rabbit-skin size, saucepan, spoons, clay bole paste

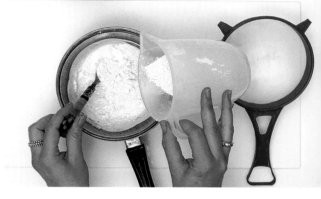

1 Sieve the whiting thoroughly. To make about 600ml/ 1 pint gesso, warm 300ml/½ pint size in a double boiler and add 620g/1lb 6oz sieved whiting, stirring gently until it has the consistency of single cream.

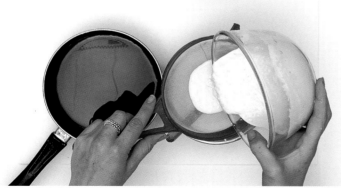

2 Sieve the mixture into another bowl to make sure there are no lumps, and keep it over a pan of warm water all the time you are using it, as it may start to gel if it cools. The gesso should be no hotter than blood heat, as any bubbles will be transferred to your work, resulting in an uneven, pitted surface.

3 To prepare the bole, place the clay in a bowl over a pan of warm water. It is easiest to add a small amount of warm size and stir in well to disperse the paste. Then add the rest of the size and stir gently. Cover the bole when not in use to keep out dust.

water-gilding

This is the pinnacle of all metallic finishes. It is definitely worth trying, although beginners may benefit from a hands-on teaching course. The technique will give tremendous satisfaction and lead you to understand why traditional gilders deserve such acclaim. It takes practice to achieve a perfectly smooth coat of gesso. If the gesso mix is incorrect the surface may flake, or the gesso may be lumpy if the whiting was not sieved. The surface may crack if the layers are too thick or have not dried between coats.

Practise picking up and applying the leaves, which blow away or fold at the slightest breath. A film of whiting on your hands and on the edge of the knife will prevent grease or moisture clinging to the gold.

The technique is fully illustrated in the Gilded Panel project, but some further advice is given below.

Materials and Equipment
wood panel, home-made gesso, saucepans and bowls, hog's hair brush, soft cloths, flat metal scraper, bole, rabbit-skin size, loose gold leaf, gilder's cushion, gilder's knife, gilder's tip, petroleum jelly (optional), gilder's mop

1 Brush on the gesso evenly. Allow each layer to semi-dry to a matt finish, then add the next. Build up at least eight thin coats, each applied in a different direction. Smooth the surface with a wet cloth, but do not overwipe. Leave to dry. Use a metal scraper to re-cut, pulling diagonally one way, then the other.

2 Apply the warm bole to the gesso surface. Leave the final coat to dry overnight. Rub down with sandpaper and clean off any dust. Add another layer if necessary. Apply each layer in a different direction, after the previous layer has dried. When dry, apply the size.

3 Transfer loose leaf from the book by blowing it out on to the cushion. Blow in the centre to smooth out. Cut with a gilder's knife. Wipe the tip across your skin to pick up a little grease to hold the gold, or use a little petroleum jelly. Touch the tip to the sheet and raise it, then touch the gold to the sized surface.

gilding with oil or acrylic size

This process can take some time and you must make sure you have a comfortable position to work in. The size can appear to be quite thick and difficult to work with so make sure you use a good brush: either flat sable or soft hog's hair brushes are best. Apply the size as thinly as possible and always take note of the recommended drying time. If you apply the leaf too soon the size will stay soft longer as the air has been excluded, and the leaf will be more susceptible to damage. The size usually appears slightly matt when it is ready to be covered. Always overlap the leaf when you apply it, to avoid obvious join lines. Dispose of any size which has been left out while working as it will have attracted dust.

Materials and Equipment

home-made or ready-mixed gesso, oil- or water-based paint, fine wet-and-dry sandpaper, 12-hour or acrylic size, loose or transfer leaf, gilder's tip (optional), gilder's knife and cushion, gilder's mop, soft cloth (optional), soft brush

1 Seal the surface with a coat of shellac and leave to dry, then build up several layers of ready-mixed gesso, applying the layers in alternate directions. Sand lightly between coats. Apply a solid coat of oil- or water-based paint to add colour and leave to dry.

2 Paint the surface with acrylic size and leave until tacky. If you are using 12-hour (oil) size, do this the day before gilding. Use a gilder's tip to lift the loose leaf and lay over the size. Tamp with a gilder's mop, held at 90° to avoid tearing, to pat out air bubbles.

3 To apply transfer leaf, hold it by the edges of the backing paper and lay it face down on the size. Rub the paper with your hand or a soft cloth. When the leaf has adhered, remove the paper, then repeat to cover the area. Brush off any loose leaf with a soft brush.

finishes for gilding

Various surface effects can be applied to gilding. Water-gilding can be burnished to a gleaming finish, but matt finishes can be produced by painting the gold with clear shellac or parchment size. It is preferable to use the opposite medium for toning to that used for sizing: for instance, it would be best to use acrylic (water-based) paints or varnish over oil-gilding. Natural wear and tear can be suggested by rubbing with wire wool to expose some of the bole beneath thr gilding. Experiment with all methods, but be careful not to destroy the adhesion of the size: allowing the correct drying time between processes is crucial.

Burnishing and distressing must not be done immediately as the gesso may still be damp, and the leaf will drag across it and tear. This is something that you will have to learn to judge for yourself, but as a rough guide it may be sufficient to gild one day and burnish on the following day.

Materials and Equipment

saucepans and bowls, clear shellac or parchment size, hog's hair brush, agate burnisher, pencil, carving tools

1 Matt the surface by adding either a coat of shellac or a thin coat of parchment size. As this is water-based it is usually applied over oil-gilding. If you do wish to wash parchment size over water-gilding, do it with one quick brush stroke to avoid disturbing the layers.

2 Use an agate burnisher to bring up a gleaming surface on water-gilding. Work gently over the area to be burnished then work back over it, gradually increasing the pressure. The burnisher should travel smoothly across the gilding, with no sticking.

3 Texture can be put into gesso to provide a relief surface to take colour and toning at the stage of patination. This can be done when the gesso is wet by making impressions with other textures. Dry gesso can be incised with a sharp metal tool.

protective finishes

Varnishes and polishes can be used both to modify the final appearance of the surface and to protect it. Although real gold leaf will not tarnish, it can benefit from the protection of a coat of clear beeswax, buffed to a subtle sheen, and aluminium leaf can be treated in the same way. Finishes such as Dutch metal or copper leaf will discolour if left exposed to the air, and need a protective coat of shellac. This finish can also be waxed if you like the soft sheen it produces.

Metallic paint effects can be waxed or varnished to seal and soften their appearance. Varnishing will deepen some colours significantly, and coloured wax can also be used to tone down the finish. If the surface is one that will receive a lot of wear – such as a tabletop or floor – you will need to build up several thin coats of varnish, sanding well between coats to give a durable finish.

Materials and Equipment
clear shellac, paintbrush, fine wet-and-dry sandpaper, clear beeswax, soft cloths, black shoe polish

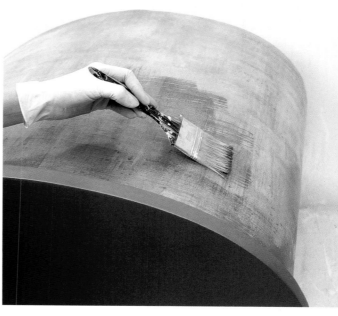

1 If you have patinated a gilded surface, seal it with shellac to prevent additional tarnishing once you have achieved the effect you want. Brush it on evenly in sections, making sure it is completely covered.

2 A painted metallic patina effect may be built up in many layers. To keep the finish slick and smooth, sand off any accumulated texture before giving the surface a layer of wax to soften the general effect and protect it.

3 Use black shoe polish to give a subtle dark sheen to metallic paint. Wipe on then buff up with a soft cloth.

metal patination

With time and exposure to air and moisture, most metal surfaces tarnish and weather in a characteristic way, producing distinctive colours and textures (such as rust on iron and verdigris on copper). This natural ageing process can be accelerated using a range of commercially available 'patinating' fluids. You can control their effects by diluting the chemicals, or limiting the time they are in contact with the metal, or you can leave the fluid to dry on the surface so that it has a continuing effect. Experiment on sample boards first to assess the effects.

Gilding, wire and metal paints can all be patinated. Bronze powders, in a range of colours, are another option: these can be brushed or patted on to a coat of size or mixed into a binder or wax, which can be applied with a brush.

Materials and Equipment

acrylic size, paintbrushes, spoon, bronze powder, patinating fluid, water spray, acrylic varnish, iron filings, matt water-based paint, PVA glue or shellac, decorator's sponges, wire wool

1 To apply bronze powder, paint on a generous coat of acrylic size and, while this is still tacky, use a spoon to sprinkle the powder over a small area at a time, then brush it into the size and leave to dry.

2 Brush on the patinating fluid lightly, working in a well-ventilated area. Dilute the fluid by misting with water, or re-apply until you have the effect you want. Seal the surface with varnish to preserve the finish.

3 Metal powders and iron filings can be combined with paint or a binder such as PVA glue and stippled on with brushes and sponges to add texture. Sponge patinating fluid lightly over the surface, and sponge off with water when the metal has oxidized. Remove excessive oxidation by rubbing with wire wool.

painted metallic effects

Highly original painted effects can be achieved by reproducing the subtle patinations and textural variations of metallic surfaces. The samples reproduced in this book give some idea of the range that is possible, but experimentation is the key, building up thin layers of paint into a durable finish full of depth and interest. Use matt paint to imitate the powdery surface of oxidized metal, forming a lively contrast with shiny, reflective metallics. Like gilded surfaces, metallic paints can be distressed and aged, toned down to a subtle sheen with translucent washes of colour and softened with wax finishes.

Materials and Equipment

primer in red oxide and black, paintbrushes, silver oil-based paint, artist's oil paints, white spirit, artist's acrylic paint in black and blue lustre

1 As with gilding, the underlying colour will influence the metallic effect. Red oxide will enhance the richness of gold or copper paint. Black primer will give silver a dark, steely look.

2 Over a base coat of silver, thin washes of oil paint in earth colours are spattered with white spirit to create an organic-looking, mottled effect with a subdued gleam.

3 Transparent washes of colour over metallic paint enhance the effect of texture and patination on a dramatic relief surface. Dilute black paint is stippled into recesses and blue lustre highlights areas of high relief.

The following pages give an indication of the wide range of finishes and effects that can be achieved with oil- or water-based paints, metal leaf, bronze powders and patinating fluids. Use the swatches for reference, experimenting with colours and applications on sample boards before beginning a decorating project. The finishes can be sealed with shellac or varnish and buffed to a gentle sheen with clear beeswax and a soft, lint-free cloth.

painted patinas

Ultramarine blue acrylic background overlaid with silver acrylic paint applied with a sponge.

Ultramarine acrylic background, overlaid with silver and burnt umber acrylic paints applied with a sponge.

Shades of blue and silver acrylic background. Acrylic silver and burnt umber paints spattered over the top.

Cobalt blue acrylic background applied with a brush and sponge, overlaid with silver acrylic paint applied with a sponge.

Oil-based silver background. Pale-orange and silver oil-based paints spattered over the top.

Oil-based silver background overlaid with a wash of gold oil-based paint, applied with a sponge.

painted patinas

Orange matt emulsion background overlaid with washes of gold and pearlescent white emulsion paints.

Green matt emulsion background overlaid with a wash of pearlescent acrylic paint and a layer of orange emulsion applied with a sponge.

Dark-blue oil-based background, spattered with white spirit, then bright blue and antique gold acrylic paints.

Blue matt emulsion background overlaid with green emulsion applied as a wash and bright gold applied with a dry brush.

Ultramarine and burnt umber acrylic paint background overlaid with silver acrylic paint sponged and spattered.

Copper oil-based background overlaid with aqua emulsion applied with a sponge, then washes of yellow-ochre acrylic paint.

Copper oil-based background overlaid with a wash of aqua acrylic paint, dribbled to imitate verdigris.

Viridian and umber acrylic paint background mixed with terracotta primer, overlaid with a wash of antique gold.

Dark green oil-based background overlaid with viridian green and antique gold acrylic paints applied with a sponge.

painted patinas

Burnt sienna acrylic background overlaid with sponged and stippled metallic gold acrylic paint.

Dark brown matt emulsion background overlaid with iridescent bronze and copper acrylic paints applied with a sponge.

Dark brown matt emulsion background overlaid with rich gold oil-based paint, which was left to dry, sanded back, then sponged over with bright gold oil-based paint.

Gold matt emulsion background overlaid with a wash of transparent green acrylic paint. Rubbed back with wire wool in a circular motion when dry.

Metallic green acrylic base overlaid with metallic blue acrylic paint applied with a sponge.

Grey matt emulsion background overlaid with silver acrylic glitter gel.

Opal matt emulsion background overlaid with interference medium in blue, green and silver applied with a sponge.

Red matt emulsion background applied as a wash, overlaid with gold oil-based paint. White spirit was sponged over the top to create texture.

Russet metallic emulsion background spattered with antique gold and black acrylic paints.

painted patinas

Cobalt blue matt emulsion background overlaid with silver and antique gold acrylic paints applied with a brush and sponge.

Red oxide matt emulsion background dry-brushed with layers of copper and gold acrylic paints.

Aqua acrylic background dry-brushed with layers of gold and copper acrylic paints.

Black matt emulsion background dry-brushed with layers of copper and aqua acrylic paints.

Ultramarine matt emulsion background overlaid with washes of iridescent silver and gold acrylic paints.

Lemon-gold matt emulsion background overlaid with washes of copper and iridescent blue acrylic paints.

Crimson matt emulsion background dry-brushed with gold acrylic paint.

Deep red matt emulsion background overlaid with sponged acrylic paint in two shades of gold.

Cerulean blue matt emulsion background overlaid with oil- and water-based silver paints.

painted patinas

Gold oil-based background overlaid with copper acrylic and aqua matt emulsion applied with sponges.

Terracotta matt emulsion background with washes of matt emulsion in pale gold, rich gold and terracotta.

Fire copper matt emulsion background overlaid with a wash of iridescent blue acrylic paint.

Green-gold emulsion background overlaid with a wash of gold acrylic paint.

Silver grey acrylic paint applied as a wash, overlaid with a wash of antique gold acrylic paint.

Taupe oil-based background overlaid with silver acrylic paint applied with a sponge. Additional layers of gold and silver acrylic paints were spattered on.

Grey matt emulsion background overlaid with copper, antique gold and blue oil-based paints applied with a sponge and brush.

Copper acrylic background overlaid with washes of iridescent red, gold and blue acrylic paints.

Biscuit matt emulsion overlaid with red and gold acrylic paint spattered on top.

painted patinas

Bright green and lemon gold matt emulsion paints applied as washes.

Green oil-based background applied as a wash, with a thick layer of antique gold applied with a sponge. The gold layer was left to dry then sanded back.

Brown-red oil-based background overlaid with antique gold applied with a sponge. White spirit was spattered over the surface and patted off with a soft cloth.

Bright green and lemon gold matt emulsion paints applied as washes.

Bronze coloured metal primer.

Dark copper oil-based background overlaid with washes of fire copper and bright gold oil-based paints.

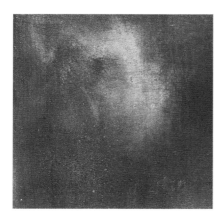

Payne's grey acrylic background overlaid with copper acrylic paint applied with a sponge.

Orange matt emulsion background overlaid with washes of red, bright copper and gold acrylic paints.

Gold oil-based background overlaid with a wash of red oil-based paint. White spirit was dribbled on to create texture, then the whole surface was varnished.

metal-leaf patinas

Copper leaf treated with green patinating fluid.

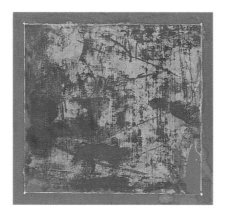

Copper powder treated with copper patinating fluid, then rubbed back with rough sandpaper.

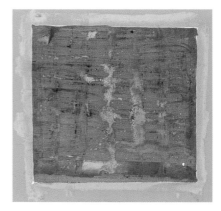

Copper powder treated with bronze patinating fluid.

White gold treated with bleach.

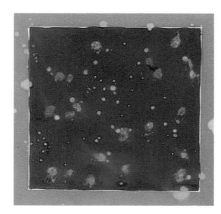

Iron filings treated with antiquing patinating fluid.

Silver leaf treated with ammonia.

Iron filings treated with rust patinating fluid.

Copper powder spattered and sprayed with patinating fluid.

Copper leaf treated with diluted ammonia.

metal-leaf patinas

Italian gold leaf over oil size, distressed with wire wool.

Dutch metal silver leaf over green base, treated with black and brown spirit dyes.

Dutch metal gold leaf over terracotta background, treated with gold spray paint.

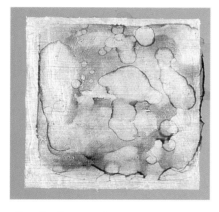

Silver leaf over pale blue background, treated with black and red spirit dyes.

Dutch metal gold leaf over terracotta background, treated with bleach.

Dutch metal silver leaf treated with bleach.

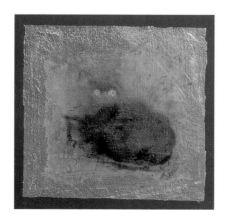

Dutch gold metal leaf over terracotta base, treated with ammonia.

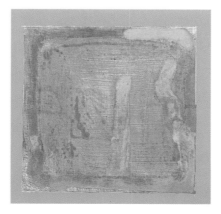

Copper leaf over yellow base, treated with bleach and patinating fluid.

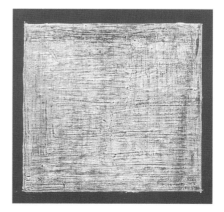

Italian gold leaf on acrylic size over a terracotta base. Sanded back after application.

patterned metallics

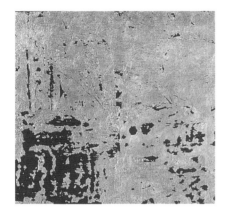

Dutch metal gold leaf applied over a base of terracotta matt emulsion. The leaf was rubbed back to reveal the background colour.

Brilliant purple matt emulsion background overlaid with metallic silver, gold and green acrylic paints applied with a sponge.

Dark brown matt emulsion background overlaid with bronze acrylic stripes applied with a brush, using masking tape as a guide.

Metallic aluminium and matt grey acrylic paints, applied in vertical stripes.

Crimson matt emulsion background overlaid with copper and fire-copper acrylic paints applied with a sponge.

Separate layers of dark and light silver and iridescent blue acrylic paints applied in loose brush strokes.

Terracotta matt emulsion background overlaid with yellow oxide and antique gold acrylic paints, left to dry then rubbed back with wire wool.

Squares of aluminium leaf applied over oil-based size on a background of ultramarine matt emulsion. Individual squares rubbed back with wire wool.

Squares of Dutch metal gold leaf applied over acrylic size in a chequered pattern on a terracotta matt emulsion background. Grid suggested by rubbing back joins with wire wool.

further information

suppliers

Clay Brothers Metal Supplies
24 The Green
High Street
Ealing
London W5 5DA
tel: 020 8567 2215
plate metal, tools and equipment
mail order service

Cornelissen and Son Ltd
105 Great Russell Street
London WC1B 3RY
tel: 020 7636 1045
artists' supplies, pigments, gilding
materials
mail order service

Falkiner Fine Papers
76 Southampton Row
London WC1B 4AR
tel: 020 7831 1151
specialist metallic papers
mail order service

Leyland SDM
The City
43–45 Farringdon Road
London EC1 M
tel: 020 7242 5791
general decorators' supplies,
gilding materials and equipment,
shellac, metallic and lustre paints

Liberon Waxes Ltd
Mountfield Industrial Estate
Learoyd Road
New Romney
Kent
TN28 8XU
tel: 01797 367 555
gilding waxes, restoration products
mail order service

Multifoil Ltd
Alphinbrook Road
Marsh Barton
Exeter
Devon EX2 8RG
tel: 01392 221255
plain and coloured aluminium foil

Ray Munn
861–863 Fulham Road
London SW6 5HP
tel: 020 7736 9876
decorators' supplies, metallic paints,
brushes, stucco plaster

John Myland
80 Norwood High Street
London SE27 9NW
tel: 0181 6709161
shellac, waxes, pigments,
rabbit-skin glue, brushes
mail order service

Paperchase
213 Tottenham Court Road
London W1P 9AF
tel: 020 7580 8496
mail order: 0161 839 1500
metallic papers and artists'
materials
stores nationwide

J. Smith & Sons (Clerkenwell) Ltd
24 Tottenham Road
Islington
London N1 4BZ
tel: 020 7253 1277
suppliers of metal, wire, mesh and
metal foil

Stuart R. Stevenson
68 Clerkenwell Road
London E3
tel: 0171 2531693
all specialist gilding materials and
equipment, pigments, artists'
materials, bronze powder,
patinating fluids
mail order service

Alec Tiranti Ltd
(shop)
27 Warren Street
London
W1 5DG
tel: 020 7636 8565
(mail order)
70 High Street
Theale
Reading
Berkshire RG7 5AR
tel: 0118 930 2775
sculptors' supplies, copper and iron
filings, patinating chemicals,
gilding materials and equipment

further reading

Practical Gilding
Peter and Ann Mactaggart,
Welwyn, Mac & Me, 1985

index

acknowledgements

This book is dedicated to Simon Le Vaillant, an inspiring artist and gilder, and to his family, who were greatly fortunate to be blessed by his endearing presence and unique talents.

I would like to express my gratitude to Judith Wetherall for past inspiration and teaching. She can be contacted for details of short courses and gilding notes at:

28 Silverlea Gardens
Horley
Surrey RH6 9BB
tel: 01293 775 024

I would like to thank the following people for their hard work and assistance with the production of this book:

My three star assistants: Emily Truss, Ana Stidever and Pascale Spall. Thank you for your enthusiasm and wonderful work, especially the long hours of preparation and wire weaving.

Ana, the best cat and dog nanny ever.

Tim France and his assistant Rosie for the photographs, which make the book so special.

Alistair McCowan for being endlessly resourceful and kind.

Jerry Kastner of K.D. Design for his encouragement and assistance with projects and props.

J. Hughes for yet more careful couriering.

Multifoil Ltd for supplying aluminium foil.

Mike Harrison of Pressing Matters for advice and printing plates.

Ahmed Sidki of Bow Wow, 70 Princedale Road, London W11 4NW for supplying props for photography.

Stuart R. Stevenson for technical advice and assistance with materials and equipment.

Home Chum for generously supplying materials.

A big thank you is due to Ahmed Sidki, Christina Barnard, Hilary Robertson and Imogen Stubbs for their support and generous offers of locations for photography. Particular thanks to Imogen, for your intuitive suggestions as always.

Finally, for the smoothest, easiest production yet, I wish to thank all at David & Charles, especially Ali Myer, Lindsay Porter, Becky Rochester and Beverley Jollands.

Very special thanks to
Imogen and family.